starting out in
poker

STEWART REUBEN

Published by Everyman Publishers plc, London

First published in 2001 by Gloucester Publishers plc, (formerly Everyman Publishers plc), Northburgh House, 10 Northburgh Street, London, EC1V 0AT

British Library Cataloguing-in-Publication Data
A catalogue record for this book is available from the British Library.

ISBN 1 85744 272 5

Distributed in North America by The Globe Pequot Press, P.O Box 480, 246 Goose Lane, Guilford, CT 06437-0480.

All other sales enquiries should be directed to Gloucester Publishers plc, Northburgh House, 10 Northburgh Street, London, EC1V 0AT
tel: 020 7253 7887 fax: 020 7490 3708
email: info@everymanchess.com
website: www.everymanchess.com

To
Dr Mahmoud Mahmood – whose technical assistance was invaluable
Peter Charlesworth – in memory of many enjoyable meals taken together

The Everyman Mind Sports series was designed and developed by First Rank Publishing
Typeset and edited by First Rank Publishing, Brighton.
Production by Navigator Guides.
Cover Design by Horatio Monteverde.
Printed and bound in the UK by The Cromwell Press Ltd

Contents

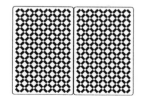

Chapter One

Poker Fundamentals

- ♣ **The Attraction of Poker**

- ♣ **The Basics of Poker**

- ♣ **The Betting System**

- ♣ **Liability**

- ♣ **The Deck**

- ♣ **Poker Variations**

- ♣ **Try it Yourself**

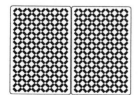

The Attraction of Poker

Poker was only introduced approximately 200 years ago. Yet, particularly in America, its terminology permeates our culture. It is used even by people who have never shuffled a deck of cards. Blue chip, four-flusher, buck and sandbagging are good examples of this. The image of hard-eyed cowboys toting pistols is indelibly engraved on the retina.

Poker is essentially a game of deception, human interrelationships and mathematical probability. Players wager on whether they have the better five cards than their opponents. Yet any businessman or politician will also run a bluff from time to time. It may not even occur to him that effectively he has been playing poker. Consider the Cuban Missile Crisis. Kennedy threatened to unleash nuclear weapons if Krushchev continued with his plan to arm Cuba. The Soviet leader backed off. Was Kennedy bluffing? Fortunately we will never know.

Chess is the great game of total information. At any stage, the position is laid out in front of you. Only your analytical ineptitude stands between you and playing the best move. Poker is much more closely related to everyday life than chess.

It is not necessary to play poker for large sums of money. I always advise newcomers to play with *less* money than they can afford to lose. They should find a group of friends who also want to flirt with the game. Then play penny ante until everybody feels comfortable. In my youth I used to play low stake poker. Now I play for thousands of dollars, but I suspect that I enjoyed playing more in those days. Of course, I enjoy winning more now, but what about the pain of losing?

When playing poker, I occasionally see players make moves of great subtlety and beauty. However, this is a far from welcome sight. Poker is about winning money. You want to play against the biggest mugs in the world, not the greatest experts.

Even the highest stake poker games are usually played with good humour and camaraderie. The image conveyed in films of snarling beasts at each other's throats lies far from the truth. I was playing poker at the Victoria Casino in London. As I left, I told the players I was going away on holiday for some time. Mansour Matloubi, the 1990 World Champion, asked me, 'Why go away when the game is here?' 'What do you think is the point of playing poker?' I enquired. 'Don't you know? It is in order to make money to play poker,' he replied. It is certainly true that the wins and losses are partly just the way of keeping score.

The Basics of Poker

- Essentially each player receives five cards.
- The players then wager on who has the best hand.
- In most forms of poker, an ace counts either as the highest card, or lowest, at the option of the player.

The following information is given in the table below: the names of the hands; their order of merit; a typical example; the number of ways the hand can be dealt from 52 cards; the odds against your being dealt such a hand or better in five cards.

There are 2,598,960 different poker hands possible, but there are only four possible royal flushes. Thus the odds against being dealt it in five cards is (2,598,960 - 4)/4 = 649,739/1.

Name	Example	Possible Hands	Odds against with 5 cards
Royal flush	A♠ K♠ Q♠ J♠ 10♠	4	649,739/1
Straight flush	9♥ 8♥ 7♥ 6♥ 5♥	36	64,973/1
Four of a kind	6♠ 6♥ 6♦ 6♣ 8♦	624	3,913/1
Full house*	Q♥ Q♦ Q♣ 4♠ 4♦	3,744	589/1
Flush	A♦ J♦ 9♦ 8♦ 4♦	5,108	272/1
Straight	5♠ 4♣ 3♣ 2♦ A♠	10,200	131/1
Three of a kind	8♠ 8♦ 8♣ 7♦ 4♣	54,912	34/1
Two pair#	J♦ J♣ 9♠ 9♥ 3♣	123,552	12/1
One pair	8♥ 8♦ Q♠ 7♠ 4♦	1,098,240	1/1 or evens
No pair	J♦ 8♣ 4♦ 3♣ 2♠	1,302,540	
Total		2,598,960	

*If two players each have a full house, the winner is decided by the higher-ranking three of a kind. Thus 9 9 9 2 2 beats 7 7 7 A A.

If two players each have two pair, the winner is decided by the higher-ranking pair. Thus Q Q 2 2 4 ('queens up') beats 8 8 7 7 A ('eights up'). Should both players have the same two pair, then the fifth card counts. Thus J J 7 7 Q beats J J 7 7 9.

There is no need to be alarmed by this table or, indeed, to remember it. Prior to writing this book, I had given no thought to these probabilities for over 20 years. I simply remembered two facts. You will be dealt a pair or better half the time. A royal flush is 650,000/1. Moreover, the latter figure is just an amusing statistic.

The Betting System

From two to ten players can take part in a game of poker. There are then two basic systems for starting play. That chosen depends on the game and the local rules.

Blinds

The players are dealt their cards. The deal rotates around the table. The dealer is indicated by a buck or button. The first player is to the left of the dealer. He is the small blind and must bet before receiving his cards, let us say $1. Usually so must the second player, the big blind, let us say $2. The third player then has the option of passing, calling $2 or raising. The fourth player then also has the option of passing, calling or raising. The action then goes around the table until it gets back to the small blind. He now reacts to the previous action. The big blind then has an option. Indeed it is possible that he has won the pot because everybody has passed. If nobody has raised, he can simply check or raise himself. To check means that the player takes no action. He reserves the right to pass, call or raise later, if other players bet.

The action proceeds around the table until everybody left has put in the same amount of money. The hand then goes on to the next stage.

Example 1: The raise is limited to $2 (limit)

Player A $1 blind. B $2 blind. C passes. D calls $2. E calls $2 and raises $2. F passes. G calls. H calls $4 and raises $2. A passes. B calls $4. D calls $4 and raises $2. E calls $4. G passes. H calls $2. B calls $2. The pot now stands at $37. The hand proceeds to the next stage with B, D, E, H still in the pot. If that is the conclusion of the action, the four players show their hands. The best one wins the pot of $37. His profit will be $29.

Ante

Everybody puts the same amount of money (the ante) in the middle. This sum forms the initial pot. If there are eight players and the ante is $1, then the pot is $8. The players are dealt their cards. The deal rotates around the table of eight players. The dealer is indicated by a button. The first player to act has the option of checking or betting. In most games a player cannot check initially. He must either pass or bet a minimum stipulated sum.

Example 2: The raise is limited to the size of the pot (pot limit)

The minimum bet is $1. Player A passes. B bets $1. C passes. D calls

$1 which makes the pot size $10. He then raises $10. Players E, F and G pass. H calls $11. B calls $10 and raises $30, although he could have raised $41. D passes. H calls $30. The pot now stands at $101 and proceeds to the next stage with only B and H still in the pot.

The 'blinds' hand could equally have been pot limit and the 'ante' hand limit. It is also possible to play *no limit*. This is where the player can bet up to all the chips in front of him. He can do this at any stage, when it is his turn.

Do not assume no limit must be the biggest form, pot limit next and limit smallest. It all depends on the size of the ante and the number of betting intervals. The largest game I have ever seen was $2000, $4000 limit Seven Card Stud in 1979. I have seen pot limit played with penny antes and the players have had a fine time. They may even have been better players than those who were involved in the much bigger game at the next table.

Liability

You are always only ever liable to lose the money you have on the table in front of you. It is normal to stipulate a minimum amount with which you must start. With blind betting this is typically 40 times the big blind. In pot limit it is often 100 times the ante. With the ante at $1, then you must start with at least $100. If you are losing, then you can continue playing until you run out of money. If you are winning, you cannot remove money from the table while you are still in the game. This is known as 'weeding' in England and 'going South' in America. It is against the rules. You cannot add to your stake in the middle of a hand. If you wish to add money, it must be done before the new hand is started.

There is absolutely no basis in the myth that your opponent can raise you out of the pot. The film *Big Deal at Dodge City* is a perfect example of this nonsense. The hero is raised several thousand dollars. He cannot meet this and has a heart attack. His wife then raises money from the town banker, using the quality of the hand as collateral.

Example 3: Players A and B have $200 and player C only $50

The pot size may reach $150, $50 from each player. This is called the main pot. A and B can bet a further $150 each on the side. This is a side pot. C can only win the main pot of $150. Only A or B can win the side pot of $300.

I once had the pleasure of setting in the other seven players at the table and winning. This resulted in several side pots, all of which I won. I only held a flush.

The Deck

A standard deck has 52 cards, there are four suits and 13 different cards. Counting a king as 13, queen 12, jack 11 and ace as 1, the total point count comes to 364. It cannot be a coincidence that there are 52 weeks in the year, 4 seasons, 13 lunar months and 365 days.

Have you ever noticed that you can see only one eye of the J♠ and J♥? Hence the expression, 'One-eyed jacks'. The K♦ is also similarly portrayed. The other nine court cards gaze on us through both eyes.

Poker Variations

There are many ways in which poker can be played and new ones are being invented all the time. No single game is best. Everybody has their personal preferences and from time to time a new game becomes popular. This is often created partly with the idea of confusing the unwary. Hold 'Em and Seven Card Stud are the most popular variations. Much of the rest of this book is concerned with the different forms. Do read every chapter. Some concepts are universal, but are best explained with reference to a particular type of poker.

Try It Yourself

1. Which hand would you prefer to have, a straight or flush?

2. How frequently will you hold a pair or better in five cards?

3. The pot is $10. Player 1 bets $10. Player 2 calls. How much can Player 3 raise in pot limit?

4. How many cards are there in a standard deck?

5. What is the most you could conceivably lose in a hand?

Answers on Page 151.

Chapter Two

Draw Poker

- ♣ The Rules of Draw Poker

- ♣ Basic Strategy

- ♣ Drawing Hands

- ♣ Weighing up the Odds

- ♣ Play after the Draw

- ♣ Bluffing

- ♣ Try it Yourself

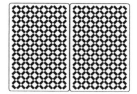 

Recently a beginner asked me a question about Draw poker. I realised that my answer virtually encapsulated the whole of the game of poker. Thus we shall begin with this variation. It is certainly the game I played when I started out.

The Rules of Draw Poker

- Each player is dealt five cards.

- There is a betting interval, until all the players left in have wagered the same sum.

- Then each player discards from zero to five cards, starting with the player first in hand.

- Each is given the same number as they have discarded by the dealer from the cards remaining in the deck.

- If there are insufficient cards to go around, the discards are shuffled and used again.

- There is then a second betting interval, until all the players left in have wagered the same sum.

- The cards are then shown and the best hand wins.

The player to show first is either the last one to bet or the first after the dealer. I prefer the former. After all, when a player calls, he is 'seeing' the last bet. Theoretically all hands should be shown at the end. Many players seek to hide what they had in order not to give any clues to their strategy. I never object to showing my own hand. I usually do not want to see that of my opponent. He may have made a mistake and was, after all, winning the hand. If there is a bet and no call, the only player left is under no obligation to show his hand.

Example 1: Limit

The above diagram represents a table with the six players and their hands. The dealer is at '11 o'clock', i.e. between Ali and Joe. The action takes place clockwise around the table.

The game is limit raise. The initial pot is $6, $1 being anted by each of the six players. The bet or raise before the draw is $1 and $2 after.

Joe is first to speak and checks. Sid bets $1. Ann calls. Hal raises $1. Tom passes. Ali calls. Joe passes. Sid and Ann call. The pot is $14.

Sid takes three cards and ends up with (A♥ A♣ K♥ K♣ 2♣). Aces up.

Ann takes one card and ends up with (K♠ Q♦ J♥ 10♥ 9♣). King high straight.

Hal takes one card and ends up with (9♠ 9♦ 3♠ 3♣ A♦). Nines up.

Ali takes three cards and ends up with (8♥ 8♣ 8♦ 5♠ 3♥). Trip eights.

Sid checks. Ann and Hal check. Ali bets $2. Sid calls. Ann raises $2. Hal passes. Ali calls. Sid passes. Ali and Ann show their cards and Ann wins a pot of $24.

As we shall see, Ali should never have been in the pot in the first place. He lost the most. Ann trap-checked and this probably netted her $4 more than a straightforward bet.

Example 2: Pot limit

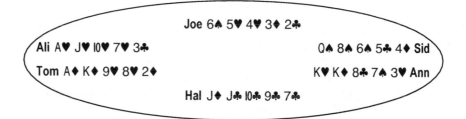

Each player again antes $1 so that the pot is $6. Sid is first to speak. It would be unfair if Joe always had to open. Sid checks. Ann bets $5. Hal calls. Tom passes. Ali calls. Joe calls $5 and raises $20. Sid passes. Ann passes. Hal calls. Ali calls. The pot is $86.

Hal takes one card and ends up with J♣ 10♣ 9♣ 7♣ 6♣.
      Jack high flush.

Ali takes one card and ends up with A♥ J♥ 10♥ 7♥ 6♥.
      Ace high flush.

Joe stands pat (takes no cards).
      Six high straight.

Hal and Ali check. Joe bets $80. Hal calls. Ali raises $200. Joe passes. Hal calls. Ali wins a $726 pot with the better flush.

Hal broke his pair of jacks to try to make a flush. Note, his drawing potential was high. He can make a straight with an eight, and a straight flush with 8♣. Both Hal and Ali checked to Joe. He would have spoilt their game, had he also checked. Once both players acted, he knew that at least one of them must have his little straight beaten.

Returning to the conversation I had at the start of this chapter, the question posed was, 'Should I draw two cards or three to a pair?'

Obviously you are more likely to improve to three of a kind (trips), a full house or four of a kind (quads) if you take three cards. You are actually marginally *less* likely to make two pair if you draw the maximum. This is because you may draw the same denomination cards as you threw away. Thus you hold J♦ J♥ A♠ 9♣ 2♦. What if you throw away only the two small cards? Then you are much more likely to make the powerful two pair, aces up. You will, however, be fresh out of luck if one of your opponents started with aces.

Thus you draw two cards rather than three in order to be deceptive. Your opponent may decide that you have trips rather than just a pair. This subtlety will be totally wasted if your opponent is so inexperienced that he does not notice.

WARNING: Never try to be fancy against a weak player.

If you have bet or raised, your hand is unlimited. You may have anything from no pair to a royal flush.

NOTE: You can bet with any hand.

If somebody else has bet, then you must surely have some sort of hand if you call.

TIP: If you call, you must have a hand of some value.

If you call somebody else who bets, the inference is that your hand is not very strong. Thus, if you call and take two cards, your opponents are unlikely to believe you had trips. With such a good hand, you should normally raise.

You start with K♥ K♦ 8♣ 7♥ 4♦. A player bets and most other players fold. Now you raise. The opener is the only caller and takes three cards. You just take two. He may well pass a bet after the draw even if he makes two pair aces up.

However, let us suppose you started with A♠ A♥ A♦ 7♣ 4♦. Somebody bets, you call and then take two cards. A fairly strong opponent is likely to believe you only have a pair. It is much more likely he will call after the draw. You may improve to an absolute monster and trap an opponent who also improves. This is important in pot limit, but much less so in limit. A really strong opponent will come to know that you are capable of playing so deceptively.

TIP: It seldom pays to try to outwit a really strong player. You should try to avoid being at the same table as such opponents. If they are unavoidable, try to avoid confrontation and pick off the fish in the game.

Now you will understand why, when I gave this answer to my novice friend, he said, 'Thank you. I think I will be able to win now.'

Basic Strategy

Your minimum opening hand should be a pair of jacks. This is because the average two pair is jacks up, for example, J♥ J♦ 7♣ 7♠ 9♥. This is so much so that, in many Draw poker games, the minimum hand to initiate action is a pair of jacks or better.

The earlier in the hand you have to act, the stronger your hand needs to be. If you act late, everybody may have thrown away their hand before it ever reaches you. Also, if you are last to speak before drawing cards, then you will also be last to act after the draw. If everybody has passed and you are the penultimate player, then any pair is good enough to bet. Even an ace high is correct strategy. The last player has nothing 50% of the time. It is suicidal to open first in hand with just jacks in an eight-handed game.

If somebody else has opened and he plays the same strategy as you, then his minimum hand is a pair of jacks. Naturally in real life he may be bluffing or have had a rush of blood to the head. Of the 2,598,960 possible five card hands (see Chapter 1), 536,100 are a pair of jacks or better:

Two pair or better	198,180
Aces or better	282,660
Kings or better	367,140
Queens or better	451,620
Jacks or better	536,100

If the antes were $8 and your opponent has bet $2, then you are wagering $2 to win $10. This is 5/1. Your hand should be in the top 536,100 x 5/6 = 446,750 to call. You need at least a pair of queens.

If the antes were $8 and he has bet $8, then you only have 2/1. Thus your hand should be in the top 536,100 x 2/3 = 357,400 to call. Now kings are a marginal call.

I cannot believe that anybody really thinks like this when at the poker table. However, it would be logical for a computer. Instead a player might carry a ready-reckoner in his head of what each action means.

In the following table, 'Facing raise cold' means that you have taken no action in the pot yet. Thus you have to cover both the original bet and the raise. Note that X X represents a pair of undefined denomination.

Minimum to	Limit		Pot Limit	
	Call	Raise	Call	Raise
Taking first action	JJ		JJ	
Facing bet	QQ	AA	KK	77XX
Facing raise as bettor	AA	JJXX	KKXX	777
Facing raise cold	88XX	222	AAXX	Trip 10s
Facing 2nd raise as bettor	call	222	AAA	A Flush
Facing 2nd raise cold	777	AAA	KQJ109	333XX

To proceed any further than the second raise is pure conjecture. In pot limit, at least one player will run out of chips by this stage. This is called being 'all-in' or 'tapped'. If you raise you are rendering yourself liable to a re-raise. In pot limit you must be conservative about doing this. Raising with a hand which can improve if you buy cards (see the next section), is dangerous. If raised back, then you may have to throw your hand away. In limit this is irrelevant, since the raises are so small. You will always have pot odds.

WARNING: In pot limit or no limit, it is dangerous to raise with a hand you may wish to draw to.

In limit, a single raise will not shake anybody loose of the pot. However, a double raise may do the trick, particularly since the player considering a call knows he may face yet another raise on the next round of betting.

In limit, it is normal to allow only three or four raises when there are more than two players in the pot. This is to prevent a player being sandwiched between two players colluding. He might lose a big pot which he can never pass. No such limitation is required in pot limit. A player must expect to be liable for all his chips in any pot.

When making your decisions, you must estimate how 'tight' or 'loose' the opposition is. Against tight players, you must set higher standards, unless you think you can bluff them out. Conversely, against loose players you must lower your standards and not expect to run a bluff.

TIP: It is extremely important to gauge how your opponents play.

Tight describes a player who only plays with premium hands.

Loose describes a player who may play with weak hands.

Good players vary their play and thus sometimes play tight and other times loose.

TIP: When in doubt in limit, call. When in doubt in pot limit, pass.

Drawing Hands

Name	Example	Cards Taken	Drawing	Odds
4 card straight	9 8 7 6	1	10 or 5	5/1
4 card middle-pin straight	9 8 6 5	1	7	11/1
4 card one end straight	4 3 2 A	1	5	11/1
4 card flush	Q♠ 9♠ 6♠ 4♠	1	Spade	4/1
4 card straight flush, middle pin	8♠ 7♠ 6♠ 4♠	1	Spade or 5	3/1
4 card up and down straight flush	8♠ 7♠ 6♠ 5♠	1	Spade, 9 or 5	2/1
3 card straight flush	10♠ 9♠ 8♠	2	Straight +	11/1
A K same suit	A♠ K♠	3	Two pair +	13/1
Pair	K K	3	Two pair +	3/1
			K K K +	8/1
			Full house +	99/1
			K K K K	380/1
Pair and kicker	9 9 A	2	Two pair +	3/1
			9 9 9 +	12/1
			Full house +	125/1
			9 9 9 9	1100/1
Two pair	9 9 4 4	1	Full house	11/1
Trips	Q Q Q	2	Q Q Q × × or Q Q Q Q	9/1
			Q Q Q Q	15/1
Trips and kicker	Q Q Q 9	1	Q Q Q 9 9 or Q Q Q Q	11/1
			Q Q Q Q	47/1

In the above table '+' means 'or better'.

It is also possible to have a drawing hand rather than a made one. 9♥

8♥ 7♠ 6♣ 3♦ is such a hand. You throw away the trey (3♦). You now buy one card and hope it will be a 10 or 5 which will give you a straight. You have seen five cards so that there are 47 to come. The odds against your making the straight is (47-8)/8 = 4.875/1. We do not need to care about the exact figure, 5/1 is close enough.

If the pot is $10 and it is $2 to you to call, then you have 5/1 odds. It is correct to call. If the pot is $10 and it is $8 to you to call, then calling is a big mistake. It is much more likely that you will achieve the correct odds in a limit game than in pot limit. It is usually wrong to make only a small raise in a pot limit game. The raise indicates that you have a good hand. You are giving your opponents the odds to outdraw you. If they do so, they may win more of your money. If they fail, they will not lose any more.

It is essential to know the odds against certain draws (see table).

Weighing Up The Odds

We can hope to receive suitable odds only for four to an up and down straight or a four flush. An open-ended four card straight flush is a premium hand. It is only 2/1 against making at least a straight.

Occasionally we will accept odds of only 3/1 in order to mix up our play. To do so all the time will mark us as too loose a player. We are playing too tight if we do not accept 4/1 or 5/1 odds for these hands due to the concept of 'implied odds'.

Implied Odds

You call to make a hand such as a straight. Then you may win money after the draw. This is because, having improved, you bet and are called. There is $8 in the pot and you are facing a $2 bet with a four straight. You are receiving 4/1 for your money and it is 5/1 against. However, you call and make the straight. Now you bet $4 after the draw. When called, you win $8 + $4 = $12 and thus have received 6/1 odds.

Thus there is an implication that you can assume better odds than those currently available. The problem is that your opponent(s) may improve to a hand even better than a straight. Then you will lose even more money.

Clearly, the more players in the pot who have called, the better odds you have. However, never forget that there are then more players who have the chance of beating you. This is particularly important when trying to make a straight. Some opponents may be aiming for a flush. If they fail, then, like yourself, they fold and lose no more money. But what if you both improve? Ouch!

Some authors refer to the 'implied odds' of players in the hand who have yet to act. They may call after you and thus give you your 4/1 or 5/1 odds. This is absolute nonsense. They may raise and lead you into an even deeper quagmire. If you read this statement in a book, only continue to study it with an extremely critical mind. If an author has made one error, he may have made others. Better still, throw the book away or sell it to someone else.

Play after the Draw

In limit the bet is usually twice the size of the bet before the draw, whereas pot limit continues to be just that.

If you still just have one pair, it is best to check most of the time.

One or more opponents have called and taken one card. You should then check whatever hand you have. This may even be true if you stood pat (took no cards) yourself. If they are trying to make a straight or flush and fail, they will pass if you bet. You have gained nothing. After you check, they *may* try to bluff.

 TIP: If your opponent is drawing, leave him room to bluff.

Bluffing

It is very difficult to bluff in a limit game. The odds are just too good to be spurned. Thus it is usually only possible to bluff out a good player. One example is to raise before the draw and stand pat rather than take any cards. It is likely to be checked to you. Then bet and you have a good chance of securing the pot. This play may be successful once in an evening. What have you risked? The antes were $8. You call a $2 bet and raise $2, which is called by the original bettor. Then, after the draw, you bet $4. Thus you have risked $8 to win $10.

In pot limit again the antes are $8. The opener bets $8 and you raise $24. If he calls then, after the draw and you take no cards, you can bet $72. Now you have risked $104 to win $40. Forget the amounts and note the proportions. It is proportionately much more expensive to bluff at pot limit. However, you are also much more likely to be successful.

The most common situation is as follows. There are two players in the pot, the bettor takes three cards and the caller takes one. After the draw, the opener checks and now the caller bets. At limit the original opener will almost always call, unless he makes a full house, when he will raise. At pot limit his actions are much less clear-cut.

Imagine you took one card and bet. Now your opponent raises you and you have a flush. Could he really be bluffing that he has drawn three cards to make a full house? You must make a crying call at limit, but often pass at pot limit.

 WARNING: If your opponent represents a highly improbable hand, he probably has it.

Truly the very essence of poker is deception, but much of the outcome is decided by probability and reading people.

Try It Yourself

Each question should be answered for both limit and pot limit in an eight-handed game.

1. Should you check or open with Q Q in second position?

2. The first two players have checked, the third bet and the next three players passed. What action should you take with A A?

3. The first three players have checked, the fourth bet and you are fifth in hand. What action should you take with a four flush?

4. You opened with K K. There was one caller and you have made K K 7 7 9. You are first to speak and he took one card. What action should you take?

5. A player opened and three players called before you. You called holding 9 8 7 6 and have hit a 5. The opener takes three cards and bets, the second player calls, the third player raises having taken one card and the fourth player calls. What action should you take?

Answers on Page 151.

Chapter Three

Hold 'Em Poker

- ♣ **Rules of Hold 'Em Poker**

- ♣ **Starting Holdings**

- ♣ **Drawing Hands**

- ♣ **Strategy before the Flop**

- ♣ **Strategy after the Flop**

- ♣ **Try it Yourself**

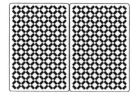 

Rules of Hold 'Em Poker

- Each player is dealt two cards face down. The deal moves to the left after each hand. There is one round of betting on these first two cards.

- The top card is now burnt. (No, not literally!) The top card is discarded unseen. This reduces the possibility of cheating or seeing the card accidentally.

- Three consecutive cards are now dealt face up in the middle of the table. These cards are known as the 'flop'. They are community cards used by every player still in the hand. There is then a second round of betting.

- Once again a card is burnt.

- After that a fourth card is dealt face up ('the turn' or 'fourth street'). This joins the other three and there is a further round of betting.

- There is a final burn card.

- A fifth and final community card is dealt face up ('the river' or 'fifth street'). A last round of betting takes place.

- Each player now has two cards in his hand and the five community cards – seven in total.

- The hand that wins is that of the player with the best five of his seven cards. A player may use both his own cards, just one, or even none at all. The latter is called 'playing the board'.

Example 1: Limit

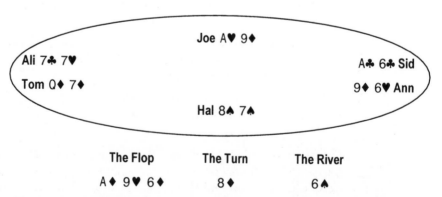

The pot was $80. Sid opens for $20 before the flop and everybody calls. The pot is $200.

On the flop, Joe has two pair aces and nines. Sid has two pair aces and sixes. Ann has two pair nines and sixes. Hal has four to an up and down straight. Tom has four to a queen flush. Ali still has just a pair of sevens. Joe checks. Sid bets $20. Ann, Hal and Tom call. Ali passes. Joe raises $20 and all call. The pot is $400.

On the turn Tom has made a flush. The others have not improved. Joe bets $40. Sid and Ann call. Hal passes. Tom raises $40 and the others call. The pot is $720.

On the river both Sid and Ann have made a full house. Joe still has just aces and nines. Tom has a flush. Sid checks. Ann bets $40. Tom calls. Joe passes. Sid raises $40. Ann re-raises $40. Tom calls. Sid caps it with the third raise of $40 and Ann and Tom call.

At the end, Sid's hand counts as A♦ 6♦ 6♠ A♣ 6♣; Ann's as 9♥ 6♦ 6♠ 9♦ 6♥; and Tom's as A♦ 6♦ 8♦ Q♦ 7♦.

Thus Sid wins a pot of $1200.

Example 2: Pot limit

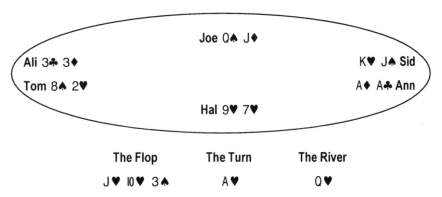

	The Flop	The Turn	The River
	J♥ 10♥ 3♠	A♥	Q♥

Being the second hand, Sid is first to speak, since Joe is the dealer. The pot is $1 and he bets $1. Ann and Hal call. Tom passes and the other two players call. The pot is $6.

After the flop, Sid is still first to act. He checks. Ann bets $3. Hal calls. Ali calls $3 (making the pot $15) and raises the maximum $15. Joe passes. Sid calls $18 and Ann and Hal call $15. The pot is $78.

Sid is still first to act on the turn. He checks. Ann also checks. Hal bets $70. Ali, Sid and Ann all decide to call. The pot now stands at $358.

On the river Sid checks first in hand. Ann checks. Hal bets $300. Ali passes. Sid calls $300, making the pot $958 and raises the whole amount. Both Ann and Hal pass. Let's see what each player had at each stage:

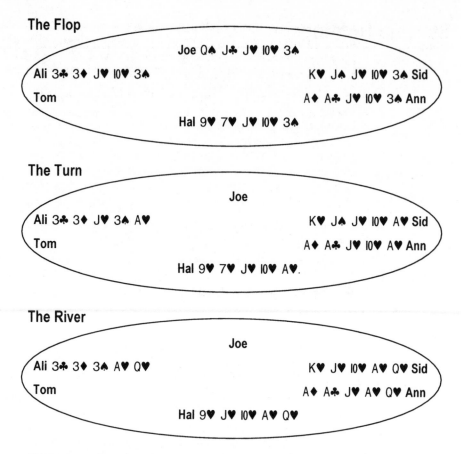

The Flop

Joe Q♠ J♣ J♥ 10♥ 3♠

Ali 3♣ 3♦ J♥ 10♥ 3♠   K♥ J♠ J♥ 10♥ 3♠ Sid

Tom   A♦ A♣ J♥ 10♥ 3♠ Ann

Hal 9♥ 7♥ J♥ 10♥ 3♠

The Turn

Joe

Ali 3♣ 3♦ J♥ 3♠ A♥   K♥ J♠ J♥ 10♥ A♥ Sid

Tom   A♦ A♣ J♥ 10♥ A♥ Ann

Hal 9♥ 7♥ J♥ 10♥ A♥.

The River

Joe

Ali 3♣ 3♦ 3♠ A♥ Q♥   K♥ J♥ 10♥ A♥ Q♥ Sid

Tom   A♦ A♣ J♥ A♥ Q♥ Ann

Hal 9♥ J♥ 10♥ A♥ Q♥

Sid has made a royal flush, using only K♥ from his hand. Since all the other players passed, he did not need show down this monster.

In both hands Sid has hit a lucky last card to win the pot. In case you are wondering, Sid was my father's name. Let's be honest though. He played like a maniac in the second example.

Remember, sometimes you may play the board. That is, use neither card from your hand. This would be the case with a winning A K Q J 10 on the table. Hole cards are now irrelevant. Everybody remaining in the pot splits it with the nut straight. Had the board been K Q J 10 9, then any player with an ace would have held the stone cold nuts. All the other players have a king high straight.

One technique is extremely important in Hold 'Em: to recognise, at a glance, what is your best hand and what is the best possible hand. I recommend that you practise this by laying down a whole series of hands and flops. Until you are confident of this, please do not put your money at risk.

TIP: The basics deserve our full attention.

Starting Holdings

Hold 'Em is an example of a community card game. Beginners often ask, 'Why is it better to start with one hand rather than another?' After all, it's possible to improve any hand.

In the game of Hold 'Em, the best hand at any stage is probably also the one most likely to win the pot. Thus a pair of aces is the best possible hand before the flop. If you start with J♦ 10♦, then you can buy a J or 10 or make a straight or flush. If you start with 7♥ 2♣, then you can only buy pairs (or trips about one hand in 100). Moreover, imagine that the flop is 7 7 2. You are unlikely to win much money, since the other players will most probably not make a decent hand. In poker you are always looking to get the money, not simply to hit the best hand.

TIP: The value of a hand is determined by how much you can win. The intrinsic value is less important.

With a flop Q♥ J♥ 10♥, you are unlikely to win much holding A♥ K♥. With a flop A♥ K♥ Q♠, you are much more likely to win money holding J♦ 10♦. You are also more likely to be outdrawn.

TIP: If you can't lose, you probably can't win much either.

Twenty-five years ago Dave Sklansky wrote an excellent book, *Hold 'Em Poker*, which provides a list of the order of merit of the Hold 'Em hands before the flop. The order depends on many factors: whether it is no limit; pot limit; or limit; whether it is cash; or tournament poker; and the particular betting structure. Only one thing is certain, in any form you would like to put all your money in before the flop with A A.

The following table lists an order of merit of the first two cards ignoring the type of game.

s is used to denote two cards of the same suit.

X stands for a card of undefined denomination.

The middle row identifies the group. The 'odds' represents the odds of receiving this hand or better.

See table on next page.

Other hands are hardly worth considering. Thus their relative merits are of no interest. If you choose to play them, effectively you are bluffing. Since nobody knows your hand anyway, what is the point of this? There is no need to saddle yourself with poor starting hands. The list contains enough choice for all your bluffs.

Hand	Gp	Odds
A A	1	220/1
K K	2	110/1
Q Q	2	73/1
A K s	2	60/1
A K	2	38/1
A Q s	3	34/1
A J s	3	31/1
J J	3	27/1
K Q s	3	25/1
A Q	3	20/1
A 10 s	4	19/1
10 10	4	17/1
K Q	4	14/1
A X s	4	12/1
K J s	4	11/1
Q J s	5	11/1
9 9	5	10/1
A J	5	9/1
J 10 s	5	9/1
K 10 s	5	8.5/1
8 8	5	8/1
K J	5	7.5/1
Q J	5	7/1
10 9 s	5	6.5/1
A 10	6	6/1
Q 10 s	6	6/1
small pair	6	5/1
9 8 s	6	5/1
8 7 s	6	5/1
7 6 s	6	4.5/1
6 5 s	6	4.5/1
5 4 s	6	4.5/1
K 9 s	7	4.5/1
J 10	7	4/1
J 9 s	7	4/1
Q 9 s	7	4/1

Hand	Gp	Odds
Q 10	7	3.5/1
K 10	7	3.5/1
10 9	7	3.5/1
9 8	7	3/1
8 7	7	3/1
7 6	7	3/1
6 5	7	3/1
5 4	7	2.5/1
A X	8	2/1
10 8 s	8	2/1
Q 8 s	8	2/1
J 8 s	8	2/1
K X s	8	1.5/1
J 9	8	1.5/1
Q 9	8	1.5/1
K 9	8	1.5/1
Q 8 s	8	1.5/1
J 7 s	8	1.5/1
9 7 s	8	1.5/1
8 6 s	8	1.5/1
7 5 s	8	1.5/1
6 4 s	8	1.5/1
4 3 s	8	1.5/1
5 3 s	8	1.5/1
J 8	9	1.5/1
Q 8	9	evens
10 8	9	evens
9 7	9	evens
8 6	9	evens
7 5	9	evens
6 4	9	evens
4 2 s	10	evens
3 2 s	10	evens
10 7	10	evens
K X	10	3/4
others	11	certain

When I had very little experience of Hold 'Em, I once played 10 7 off-suit (number 70) for a bet and raise in a pot limit game. The flop came 10 7 6. Two players were all-in before it got to me. Two more poured in their money after I raised. The person who lost most held the magnificent A J! After I won, he waxed lyrical about the quality of my play before the flop. Well, he was right of course, but he went mad after the flop. I complained to the floor-man that he had recommended it to me as a small Hold 'Em game. He replied, 'Well, so it was, until you joined in!'

Hold 'Em is usually played with blinds. Thus unlike Draw poker, only the big blind can check and enter the fray before the flop. The other players must pass, call the big blind or raise. When you are on the button (last to speak) and everybody so far has passed, you can bet with anything. To raise with such as K X is normal.

If everybody has passed and you are on the small blind, it makes little sense just to call. You might as well raise with any hand in the above list.

Naturally the list is rather coarse. It seeks to cover no limit, pot limit and limit. For example, I have moved A X s way up relative to Sklansky's original list. The implied odds if you hit a nut flush are enormous in no limit and pot limit. You will not be believed and will very occasionally come up against another flush, which will leave you in a fantastic position.

A higher-ranked hand is not necessarily favourite against one lower down the list. J 10 s (19) is a considerable underdog to A 10 (25). However, it is easier to play it in multi-way action.

Some hands spell danger rather than profit. One such is A 10. It will be all very nice if the flop is 10 10 6, but 10 8 4 is much more likely. You bet and a player looks interested. He may have a higher pair, two pair or trips. It is likely he will only go to war with you if he holds at least A 10. Even then you are only splitting the pot.

In my list more emphasis has been placed on suited connectors than some will think is justified. After all, it is difficult to make a flush. Usually you will pass your hand on the flop when only one of your cards is showing. Many flushes turn up accidentally by the backdoor (that is on fourth and fifth street). In addition a small flush is a danger hand, since your opponent may well have a higher flush.

All hands in the same group can be played roughly the same way before the flop. It matters little whether you hold A♣ J♣ (number 7) or K♦ Q♦ (number 9). The play is the same. Against little opposition, you will probably wish to raise or call a raise before the flop. You will pass a second raise at pot or no limit with either of these holdings.

Drawing Hands

You are more likely to hit a straight holding connectors than when there are gaps. With 8 7, you can hit J 10 9, 10 9 6, 9 6 5 or 6 5 4. Holding 8 6 you can only hit 10 9 7, 9 7 5 or 7 5 4.

Holdings such as 9 8, A♣ 5♣ or 4 4 are all drawing hands. It is true that 9 8 s is a marginal favourite over 4 4 all-in before the flop. However, this scenario is not going to happen. Anyway, you do not know what your opponent(s) hold. You want to be in action with such holdings only in *late* position in the hand. You certainly do not want to get too busy and pour in lumps of money on such holdings.

You may call, investing a considerable sum on a draw. Then somebody else raises even more money. If you are drawing, and make your hand, you want many people to act before you. Several people may invest money before it ever comes to innocent-looking you. If you are early to speak, and hit a monster, then it is harder to get action.

TIP: When drawing it is best to be as late in hand as possible.

If you are drawing you do not want to commit a high proportion of your money before the flop. The chances are that the board cards will have nothing to do with your two cards.

TIP: When drawing before the flop in Hold 'Em, you want to risk less than 5% of your table-stake.

Be my guest if you want to commit a higher percentage. I shan't say, 'told you so'. Remember, if you cover the table, it is the amount that your opponents can lose that matters.

Odds are a little strange. In limit, you usually have better odds to a draw than in pot limit or no limit. However, your *implied* odds are much greater in the latter forms of the game.

Strategy before the Flop

Basic strategy: play only two cards both 10 or higher, a pair, or A X s. You can become a substantial winner initially just by following this strategy. As you become more experienced you can play looser, perhaps including small suited connectors.

TIP: When learning any new poker game, first play extremely tight. This can then be your road game.

Raising rather than flat calling is often the best option when you have a tight image. Other players will fold, imagining that you have a powerful hand.

TIP: If you are first to act, you should often pass or raise rather than call. This is particularly true in limit poker.

A second raise in pot limit or no limit in a ring game suggests Q Q or better. A third raise intimates A A or K K, probably the former. Limit is quite different. There will always be pot odds for an outdraw facing a single raise. Thus it is more logical to put the heat on weak hands by re-raising. In pot limit 2/1 odds is usually too short a price to consider calling before the flop.

Let us consider aces. You are going to lose a great deal of money if there is a nasty surprise. With many bets to come there is the danger that you will either win a small pot or lose a large one. Thus your objective is to get as much money as possible in before the flop. Only with position, against one opponent, can slow-playing your aces be a good strategy. Slow-play involves just calling a bet, rather than raising. This represents weakness and keeps your opponent in the hand. In no limit, the player with aces can smother the action by raising all-in. The trouble is, everybody may then pass and the payoff may be very small.

TIP: In Hold 'Em, aces want it all-in before the flop.

Occasionally, you will be tempted to raise with a hand such as 9♣ 8♣. In pot limit or no limit, you may be re-raised and then have to pass. Otherwise you will be committing more than 5% of your money.

Frequently you will be facing a raise holding a hand such as 5 5. If the game is pot limit or no limit, you should probably pass. Either you are a small favourite or big underdog.

WARNING: Avoid situations where you are a small favourite or big underdog.

Strategy after the Flop

You are mostly on your own here. Usually a player will find that he has not hit his flop – and that includes *you*. Thus it is quite normal for everybody to check to the last raiser, who will often get the ball rolling. If the flop shows an ace or king and you do not have one of these cards, you are probably beaten. That is, unless you have struck the legendary two pair or miracle trips.

If you were the last raiser, it is usually right to bet, no matter what the flop, in order to encourage other players to fold. The more players, the less valid is this recommendation. Somebody may have stumbled into a strong hand. Even blind squirrels can hold the nuts.

In limit avoid being lured in because of seemingly good odds.

You hold 10♦ 8♣. There is $20 in the pot and the flop is J♣ 8♠ 5♣. Two players check to you and you correctly bet $2 last in hand. The first player under the gun raises $2. The pot is $26. Now you feel you must call, because you have 13/1 odds. After all you can hit an 8 or 10. five cards out of 47 is only about 8/1. The pot is now $28, and you've got two chances.

The turn shows J♣ 8♠ 5♣ 3♠. Your opponent bets $4. Oh well, it's only $4 and the pot is $32. You have 8/1 and call. The pot is $36. Note, because the size of the bet has doubled, it is easier to pass than on the flop.

Fifth street shows J♣ 8♠ 5♣ 3♠ 4♥. Your opponent bets $4. Now the pot is $40 and you are getting 10/1. Better call and keep him honest. After all, he may have held 10 9 and been trying to make a straight, or two clubs trying for a flush.

Shock, horror, sensation. He holds K♠ J♦. Somehow $12 has slipped through your fingers. Yet you were almost certain that you were losing for the last $10.

The mistake was playing in the first place with 10 8.

TIP: In limit it is often *more* important to play with premium hands.

Here are some examples of Hold 'Em hands.

You hold J♦ 9♦. The flop is A♦ 9♥ 4♦. There was just one raise before the flop and you are in late position. The original raiser bets and everybody else passes.

You can *always* raise with this hand. Either you are winning, or you have the best draw. If drawing, nine diamonds, two nines and three jacks are all probably going to help your hand. You probably have 14 outs (cards which give you the winning hand). You are favourite against A K.

If instead there had been a bet and raise before it gets to you, then watch out! One player may have A♠ Q♠ and the other K♦ 10♦. Now you can only win with a jack or nine, five cards. In limit your hand is still worth a re-raise. The original bettor may pass. Alternatively both players may call. Then, when a blank comes on the turn, they may both check to you. You can check right back and thus secure yourself a trip to the river. Your ticket has only cost half an extra bet on the flop. In pot limit or no limit nobody can prescribe the best play.

You hold 4♥ 4♣. The flop is A♦ 9♥ 4♦ just as before. There is a bet and call.

At limit you should always raise. This does not shop the business that you have a monster. At pot limit or no limit, you might slow-play your hand and just call. If a blank comes there may again be a bet and call. Now you can move right in to win a gigantic pot. This is the sort of hand in which your opponent may double you up holding A K. Yet he has no outs at all.

But, beware. If a diamond comes down on fourth street, your trips may be a sorry sight. As indeed they will be if you are facing A A or 9 9. Now you are drawing dead to 4♠ (the only card that can win you the pot). Low trips are extremely explosive. Do not be upset when you lose all your money. You have walked into a brick wall and have done nothing wrong. Lick your wounds and play on. Reserve kicking the cat until later in the evening when you go home.

You hold Q♠ J♠. The flop is J♥ 7♣ 5♥. You are first to speak. It is okay in limit to bet, check-raise or slow-play this hand. In pot limit or no limit, it is easiest to come out betting. This stops anybody getting a mystery free card. If a heart comes down it should strike fear in your own heart. If anybody raises, you can take stock. Feigning weakness by checking a moderate hand creates problems. Then you do not know whether your opponent is betting from strength or bluffing.

You hold 8♦ 7♣. The flop is Q♠ 7♦ 6♥. Somebody bets and there are two callers. The pot is substantial, there having been two raises before the flop. In limit you may decide to call, for 'value', perhaps having five outs. There would have been no problem had the hand been mucked before the flop. In pot limit or no limit, if there is just one bettor who raised before the flop, you may well call. He may hold the scrawny K♦ J♦ or some such hand, which is drawing thin.

You hold A♦ J♦. The flop is 10♥ 9♥ 3♠. You have raised in late position and there were several callers. After the flop everybody checks except one bettor before it gets to you. You may decide to call all the way unless a heart, K, Q or 8 come. Only A♠ or A♣ are appealing cards to hit. Your opponent may be beating you, but why did he not trap-check? It is quite likely that he has a drawing hand. Discretion is the better part of valour and you may prefer to pass. It is *more* likely that he is bluffing with outs in pot limit or no limit than in limit. The fact that it costs proportionately little to call in limit poker is illusory.

Hold 'Em is an extremely pure form of poker. Does your opponent have a strong hand, or is he bluffing? Other variations like Omaha or Seven Stud are much more complex. Two players can have good hands at the same time. One form of poker is not better than any other, just different.

Try It Yourself

Each question relates to a) limit; b) pot limit; and c) no limit.

1. You hold K K. You bet and there are two raises before it comes back to you. What should you do?

2. You hold 9♠ 8♣. The first person after the blinds has bet. It is a ring game. What should you do in if you are: a) next to speak; b) last to speak before the button?

3. You hold Q♠ J♠. The flop is J♦ 8♣ 6♦. There are many players in the pot and you are first to speak. What should you do?

4. You hold Q♣ J♣. The flop is 10♣ 9♣ 4♦. There are many players, one of whom has bet and another raised. What should you do?

5. You hold A♣ 4♣. The flop is J♠ 10♠ 4♦. A player bet and you called as did one other after you. Fourth street brought forth J♠ 10♠ 4♦ A♦. What do you do when facing a bet?

Answers on Page 152.

Chapter Four

Seven Card Stud Poker

- ♣ **Rules of Seven Card Stud Poker**
- ♣ **Strategy on Card Three**
- ♣ **Strategy on Card Four**
- ♣ **Strategy on Card Five**
- ♣ **Strategy on Card Six**
- ♣ **Strategy on Card Seven**
- ♣ **Playing a Short-Stack at Pot Limit**
- ♣ **Try it Yourself**

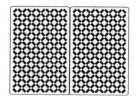 

Rules of Seven Card Stud Poker

- Each player antes one unit, perhaps $1.

- Each player is then dealt two cards face down and one face up.

- Then either the low card or high card must bet $1. In limit poker it is usually the low card, in pot limit the high card. The game is never played no limit. Sometimes two low cards of the same denomination are turned over. Then the first player after the buck must bet.

- Play then proceeds clockwise around the table as normal. A player may pass, call or raise. After this betting interval, a fourth card is dealt face up to each of the players remaining. There is another betting interval.

- Then a fifth card is dealt face up and there is another betting interval.

- Now a sixth card is dealt face up to each remaining player. There is yet another betting interval.

- Finally a seventh card is dealt face *down* to each remaining player. Thus each player receives three cards face down and four face up. There is a final betting interval at the conclusion of which each hand is shown down. The best five cards wins the hand.

- The game is played at most eight- or nine-handed.

Example 1: limit

Each player antes $1. The cards shown in brackets are those that each player has in the hole. They are thus visible only to him until the showdown.

Joe (A♣ A♦) 9♠

Ali (A♥ 6♠) 3♦

Tom (9♣ 6♣) 5♣

(10♦ 8♦) 7♣ Sid

(Q♣ J♣) 10♣ Ann

Hal (7♠ 7♦) 4♥

Hal has to bet $1. Tom calls. Ali passes. Joe raises $1. Sid passes. Ann calls. Hal and Tom call. The pot is $14.

Fourth Street (or The Turn)

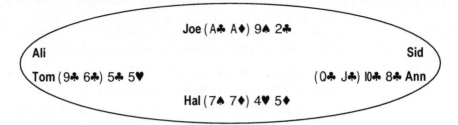

Joe (A♣ A♦) 9♠ 2♣

Ali

Sid

Tom (9♣ 6♣) 5♣ 5♥

(Q♣ J♣) 10♣ 8♣ Ann

Hal (7♠ 7♦) 4♥ 5♦

There is an open pair, so the bet can be $2. Tom is high and can check, bet $1 or $2. He chooses $1. Joe raises $2 and Ann re-raises $2. Hal calls and Tom passes. Joe re-raises $2. Ann and Hal call. The pot is $36.

Fifth Street

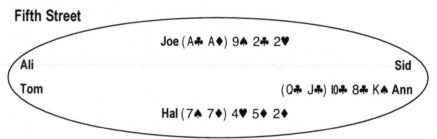

Joe (A♣ A♦) 9♠ 2♣ 2♥

Ali

Sid

Tom

(Q♣ J♣) 10♣ 8♣ K♠ Ann

Hal (7♠ 7♦) 4♥ 5♦ 2♦

Joe is high. From fifth street on the bet is always $2. Joe bets $2. Ann and Hal call. The pot is $42.

Sixth Street

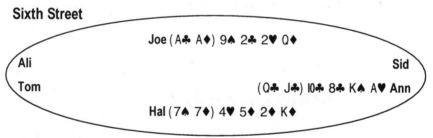

Joe (A♣ A♦) 9♠ 2♣ 2♥ Q♦

Ali

Sid

Tom

(Q♣ J♣) 10♣ 8♣ K♠ A♥ Ann

Hal (7♠ 7♦) 4♥ 5♦ 2♦ K♦

Joe is first to speak and bets $2. Ann raises $2. Hal calls. Joe calls. The pot is $54.

Seventh Street (or The River)

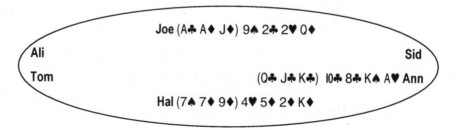

Joe (A♣ A♦ J♦) 9♠ 2♣ 2♥ Q♦

Ali

Sid

Tom

(Q♣ J♣ K♣) 10♣ 8♣ K♠ A♥ Ann

Hal (7♠ 7♦ 9♦) 4♥ 5♦ 2♦ K♦

Joe is first to speak and checks. Ann bets $2. Hal raises $2. Joe passes. Ann raises $2. Hal re-raises a further $2 and Ann raises $2. Hal raises yet again. This could continue indefinitely until a player rounds out of money. The number of raises is unlimited if there are only two players left. However, Ann just calls. The pot is $78.

Ann holds K♣ Q♣ J♣ 10♣ 8♣. Hal holds K♦ 9♦ 7♦ 5♦ 2♦. Thus Ann has the better flush and wins the pot.

There are lessons to be learnt from this hand. Hal would have saved a great deal of money had he passed on the fourth card. He suffered from the syndrome, 'Oh, another dollar won't hurt.' It was not too late on the fifth card either. However, he would have been a hero, had Ann not made her flush on the river.

Tom behaved sensibly. He bet $1 on fourth street and passed when three players clearly indicated that they believed they were holding better hands than him.

Joe started out with the best hand. He must have guessed he was losing on sixth street. However, the raise was only $2 and he would win $54 if he made a full house. He has odds of 27/1. He still had two chances to improve, A♠ and 2♠. He has seen 18 cards. Thus, as far as he is concerned, there are 34 cards to come. Two wins out of 34 is 16/1. Thus his pot odds are perfectly satisfactory. Remembering the passed cards is an important skill in this game.

TIP: It is important to remembering the passed cards at Stud.

When you play limit poker, you will find that the pot is simply heaped in the middle. Thus you will not be able to determine its size at a glance. You must make an estimate. You could ask for the pot to be counted. The last time I did that in Vegas in 1979, everybody at the table grumbled. Anyway, you will normally be calling!

Example 2: Pot limit

The total ante is $2 and the low card must bring it in (bet) $1.

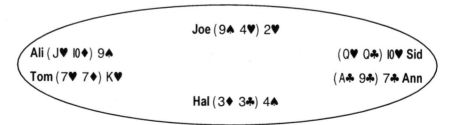

Joe has to bet $1. Sid calls. Ann calls $1 and raises $5. Hal, Tom and Ali call for $6 each. Joe passes. Sid calls $5 and raises $20. Ann calls. Hal passes. Tom and Ali call. The pot is $113.

Fourth Street

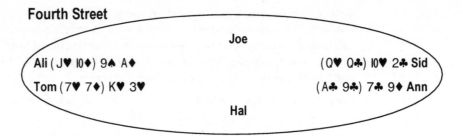

Joe

Ali (J♥ 10♦) 9♠ A♦   (Q♥ Q♣) 10♥ 2♣ Sid

Tom (7♥ 7♦) K♥ 3♥   (A♣ 9♣) 7♣ 9♦ Ann

Hal

Ali is high card and checks as do all the players. The pot remains at
$113.

Fifth Street

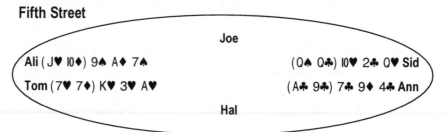

Joe

Ali (J♥ 10♦) 9♠ A♦ 7♠   (Q♠ Q♣) 10♥ 2♣ Q♥ Sid

Tom (7♥ 7♦) K♥ 3♥ A♥   (A♣ 9♣) 7♣ 9♦ 4♣ Ann

Hal

Tom bets $100. Ali passes. Sid and Ann call. The pot is now $413.

Sixth Street

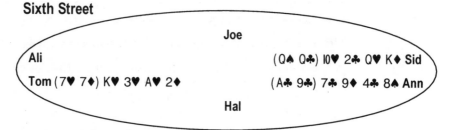

Joe

Ali   (Q♠ Q♣) 10♥ 2♣ Q♥ K♦ Sid

Tom (7♥ 7♦) K♥ 3♥ A♥ 2♦   (A♣ 9♣) 7♣ 9♦ 4♣ 8♠ Ann

Hal

Tom checks. Sid bets $250. Ann and Tom call. The pot stands at
$1163.

Seventh Street

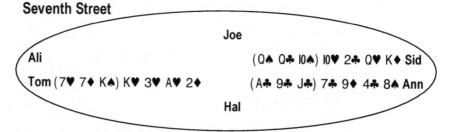

Joe

Ali   (Q♠ Q♣ 10♠) 10♥ 2♣ Q♥ K♦ Sid

Tom (7♥ 7♦ K♠) K♥ 3♥ A♥ 2♦   (A♣ 9♣ J♣) 7♣ 9♦ 4♣ 8♠ Ann

Hal

Tom checks. Sid checks. Ann bets $1,000. Tom passes. Sid raises
$3,000. Ann and Tom pass. Sid wins a pot of $3,163 without having to
show his hand.

Again there is a great deal to be learnt from this hand. Ann's $5 raise with a three flush went on to magnify the pot immensely. Try tracing through the size of the pot without that $5 raise. Once Sid raised $20, everybody else should have passed. He tempted them in by betting less than the pot.

Everybody quietened down on fourth street. Clearly Sid felt everybody had hit scare cards.

Sid has hit trip queens on fifth street, but Tom has hit an overlay – a possible flush. Ali sensibly passes. He can only make a straight with a middle-pin eight. That may already be losing to Tom. Ann makes a major error in calling. She could be drawing dead to Tom's hand. Was she feeling flighty after winning the previous hand?

On sixth street Tom realises he is not going to buy the pot with a bluff and so checks. Sid is still a little frightened, but does not wish to give a free card. He bets $250, perhaps not a good move. He is revealing that he is strong, but laying himself open to a check-raise from Tom. However, it works out well and two players call. Again Ann should have passed. She does not have adequate odds. Had she passed, so would Tom. Once she calls, he has good pot odds.

On the river Tom realises that if he bets, nobody will call with a hand worse than kings up. Thus he checks. Sid should bet, but he checks, risking not getting paid off, trying to trap Ann. This is an error. Tom might have trap-checked an ace flush and be intending to raise.

Now Ann correctly bets her hand. After all, both players have shown weakness. Tom passes. When Sid raises, Ann realises that calling would be throwing good money after bad. She passes. Note that had Sid bet $1,000, Ann would have called or possibly even raised. Thus he would have won at least the same sum of money.

Truly, poker is a game of mistakes. However, unlike most other activities, sometimes you are actually rewarded for bad play.

Strategy on Card Three

Basic Holding

Play only with trips, a pair, three to a flush or three to an up and down straight. Last in hand, you need very little if you are up against only the forced bet. To play with an ace or such as J 10 8 is fine. You can raise with any old rubbish you like. Take care of all rushes of blood to your head holding at least a king. Yes, I am recommending raising with (K 2) 7.

TIP: You need good cards to call in any game but you can raise with junk.

Three Flushes and Three Straights

You want callers when you have three to a flush or straight. The more people in the pot when you make your hand, the better chance of being called. Thus raising card three with such a hand constitutes a bluff. It is 3/1 against making a four flush. However, don't despair. It is roughly even money against a four flush or pair. You do not want to get involved in calling a double raise with a three flush, even in limit.

Pair

A concealed pair is much better than if they are split. Thus (9 9) 3 is superior to (9 3) 9, since an explosion may occur if you hit mystery trips, as in the last hand. Also if you make (9 9) 3 3, then your opponents are more likely to pass a bet. They may believe you for trips if you pair your door card. Basically this is what you want when you are holding two small pair.

The third card with your pair is much more important in limit than pot limit. 7♦ 7♣ A♥ or 7♦ 7♣ 8♦ are better holdings than 7♦ 7♣ J♠. In pot limit secondary aspects of your hand may never arise. You may need to commit too much of your money before they become important.

It is correct to make the first raise if no more than two cards showing beat your pair. For example, you hold (J 7) J. The low card has brought it in, (? ?) Q calls. Among other players, (? ?) A has yet to act. You raise. Everybody passes to the queen who raises. Now it is correct for you to call at limit and probably to pass at pot limit. In limit you have probably isolated yourself with the best hand. In pot limit you have spent money and have nothing to show for it. You have lost your chance for an outdraw. You may even have been bluffed out. All true, but you have found out early and may possibly have escaped cheaply.

Low pairs must be played cautiously at limit and probably not at all at pot limit. There is little merit in taking a hand such as (3 7) 3 up against two active higher cards. Even against one, discretion is the better part of valour. (3 3) 7 is marginally better because of the implied odds. At pot limit the odds offered for hitting mystery trips next card are poor.

In limit players often slow-play buried aces or kings. Look what happened to Joe when he kept on raising in our first example. The pot became too big for him to pass. Aces or kings are likely to win small or lose big in limit. In pot limit you can protect your high hands or throw them away if the going gets rough.

Trips

In both limit and pot limit it is often best to slow-play such hands. If you play the hell out of them, you may find yourself a little lonely. Obviously this risk is relatively slight at limit.

Strategy on Card Four

Junk

Muck your junk as rapidly as possible in pot limit. In limit your prime consideration is what to do with a hand such as (Q♣ 10♣) 7♣ 4♦. This deserves to go to the great poker graveyard – unless there were three raises on card three. My next question is – how did you let yourself get involved? Oh well, it happens and you will have to take off a card now by calling. Just pray that no third party raises.

One Pair

In limit if there has been no change with the latest card, generally you should continue as before.

For example, (7♦ 7♣) Q♥ 3♦ against (? ?) 9♠ 5♥. The low card bet card three. The nine raised before it got to you. It was perfectly okay to play, although you could also have passed. Card four it is probably better to check. You have already shown weakness by not raising from the off. If he checks right back, you have given a free card. However, you are getting a good picture of the hand cheaply. If he bets, you should call. He may be bluffing or, more likely, has a pair of nines.

Same hand, but you raised on card three and the nine called you. Now you should bet again. A three flush may have broken off. For all your opponent knows, you have a pair of queens. If he raises you, he should have queens beaten.

Now let us consider pot limit. In the above example, you probably passed a pair of sevens when the nine raised. If you called, now check and if your opponent bets, it is correct to pass or raise. Calling would be mediocre play. At least by raising you are making a play for the pot.

If you raised first and were called, bet again. You are bluffing. But, your opponent's hand may have broken off. If he calls with a pair of nines, you may improve. This is called 'bluffing with outs'. In this case you have eight cards to improve your hand. The problem is that any improvement could get you into deep trouble. If he raises, that's easy. Throw that junk away.

Whenever you check with a mediocre hand and your opponent bets, you have a problem. You do not know whether he is strong or just trying to take the pot away from you.

 WARNING: Whenever you check and your opponent bets, you will not be able to gauge his strength accurately.

Hitting an Open Pair

You should nearly always bet unless there is another open pair. The only exception is where you had to bring it in (start the betting) as low card.

In limit you usually have the option of either betting $1 or $2. Why not try just $1 occasionally? You can do it with either a good or bad hand. If the former, you are enticing people in. If the latter, you are saving money. I played that way against the late Stu Ungar (three-times winner of the World Series of Poker) once. He had said call before he even noticed that I had only bet $100, not $200 and then did a double-take, a look of surprise coming over his face. I had trip deuces and had set him up for a check-raise on the fifth street. Unfortunately he immediately hit open jacks and it came to nothing – well, at least I had saved $100.

Holding Two Pair

Take for example (9♠ 6♥) 9♦ 6♠. In pot limit it is usually best to bet or raise, rather than slow-play this hand. You will be happy if everybody passes. Your hand is not that terrific, even though it is only 3/1 against making a full house by the river.

In limit two-handed you may decide just to call a $1 bet. Then, when your opponent bets $2 on fifth street, you can raise $2 and thus gain $1. Had you raised $1 on fourth street, it is unlikely that he would have passed. Then he will check fifth street and call or pass your $2 bet.

Also your action is deceptive. Your hand may become (9♠ 6♥) 9♦ 6♠ J♦. Your raise fifth street may lead your opponent to think that you have a four flush or J J 9 9. Now, if you hit a six, he is less likely to be frightened. If you hit a diamond or a jack, he may throw away a better hand. If you hit a blank, he may think that you are very weak. Poker is all about deception.

Holding Trips

Do not be scared of betting out with low trips. If everybody passes, they probably had nothing. You might as well get on with the game. High trips can be slow-played, but you may fail to win as much money.

Recently I had (Q Q) Q Q. It is 20,824/1 against quads in four cards. I have been playing Four Card Omaha for 14 years. Fortunately, I have never had quads dealt to me. On this occasion I was up against just one opponent with an ace showing. I bet most of the pot. He called. Neither of us improved. I checked and he bet. I called. On sixth street I again checked and he bet. I raised him all-in, which he called. Had I checked on fourth street, however bad a player he is, he would have smelt a rat.

Drawing Hands

A four flush is at least as good a hand as a pair of aces. The flush only makes it 48% of the time, but there are other ways to win the pot. In limit, the four flush is *better* than aces, since your opponent is probably stuck with calling all the way. You can always pass on the river with no hand.

A four flush is obviously a better holding than a four straight. A flush is a better hand than a straight. There are nine improving cards for a flush and only eight for a straight. The weaker hand does have an advantage at pot limit. Players will not necessarily believe you when you make it. Thus the implied odds can be greater.

If your board is such as 9♥ 8♥ the potential overlay is enormous. Any heart or card queen through five may leave your opponent petrified at pot limit. Thus it is worth a bet. After all, you had something on card three. In limit it is also even worth a raise. You are staking $1,or $2 if he re-raises. When you hit your scare card fifth street, he will probably check. Then you can take off a free card if that suits you. This saves a $2 bet at the probable cost of $1.

If you have a four flush and are bet at, you do not necessarily want to re-raise. Potential callers will probably pass and this is not usually what you want.

TIP: Suited leaners showing, such as 7♦ 6♦ are a hand at Seven Stud.

Seven Stud can become quite mechanical eventually. However, initially it seems frighteningly complex. It is best to be cautious while you are still inexperienced.

Thus you have your four flush. If an opponent has an open pair, then he has a potential full house. You may make your flush, only to have it turn to ashes when he declares a full house.

You have four to an up and down straight. A player bets and somebody calls with two clubs showing before you. The tight play is to pass.

You hold (A A) Q 3. (? ?) 9 9 bets and (? ?) 2 6 calls. The opener may just have a pair of nines, but surely the caller must have that beaten. In pot limit you should pass, whereas in limit you could even raise! Leaning on the players may cause the weaker one to pass.

TIP: There is no shame in passing, especially in pot limit.

Strategy on Card Five

The bet doubles here in limit. Thus it is now time to slough off your mediocre holdings. The pot is $15 and it is only $2 to you? True, but it costs you $4 to reach the river. It will cost you another $2 to ford it once you improve and feel you have to call. That is $6 to win $21 or 3/1.

One Pair

Consider (7♦ 7♣) Q♥ 3♦ 2♠ against (? ?) 9♠ 5♥ K♣. The low card brought it in (had to bet). Before it reached you, the nine raised. There is nothing wrong with calling, nor anything wrong with passing. Card four you checked and he bet, so you called. Card five he bets the pot. It is usually best to pass.

Continuing with the same hand. This time you made the first raise and the nine called. Card four you bet out and he called obstinately. Card five he is high and checks. It would be a crime not to bet. If you check, you may be giving a free card to no advantage – a venal sin in poker. If he raises, he has a strong hand. You should usually pass. Do not regret losing that free card. Your hand was very weak.

WARNING: Do not give away free cards without good reason. It is more generous than a soft call.

TIP: Being the aggressor puts you in the driving seat. Buckle up and play.

If checked, our pair of sevens should be ditched if your opponent bets. If he also checks, get ready to check it down (unless you improve). Then hope your mediocre holding will stand up.

Holding (A♠ 9♦) A♥ 6♠ 4♦ against (? ?) J♦ 7♠ 8♥.

You have bet throughout. You should do so again. It is true that he may have hit a straight on fifth street but it is unlikely. In limit you *must* bet again. In pot limit you may judge it wiser to check. As usual, once you check and he bets, you have no idea who is winning. If you check and just limply call, you have probably made a mistake.

Holding Two Pair

For example, (9♦ 4♥) 9♥ 7♠ 4♦ against (? ?) A♣ 3♦ J♠.

Whether at limit or pot limit, this hand deserves a raise when the ace bets. If you are petrified of aces up, then why did you call on fourth street?

Holding Trips

Normally you still have a terrific hand. You need only be wary against an open three flush or open pair. (? ?) J♥ 2♦ J♠ is much more frightening than (? ?) 2♦ J♥ J♠. He is much more likely to have trips with the former hand.

Take the example of (9♠ 9♦) Q♣ 4♥ 9♣ against (? ?) 7♦ J♦ 2♦. At limit you can bet and call a raise. At pot limit you will probably prefer to check. That is, unless you have good reason to believe that the flush is not there. If your opponent bets, it is rarely correct to pass. The chance of making a full house is just too good to pass up, even at pot limit.

With (A♠ A♥) 7♦ A♦ X it is a good idea to bet or raise. Your opponent may put you on a four flush. Next card, you hit an apparent blank. Now he may get terribly involved in a dreadful position.

Other Holdings

A holding such as (9♠ 4♠) Q♠ 7♠ 9♦ is a good hand against an opponent whose holding is not threatening. Certainly raise at limit with this hand. Pot limit? Well, it partly depends on how much heart you have.

Now consider (A♦ 4♥) A♣ 9♠ Q♥ against (? ?) 3♠ 6♥ 6♠ and (? ?) 9♣ 4♠ 2♣. The open pair bets and the 9 4 2 calls. It is correct to raise or pass at limit. The pair of sixes will probably re-raise and the 9 4 2 pass. Now you have isolated yourself with the best hand. It has been costly, but stragglers must never be invited to the party. A call on fifth street would have been poor technique. At pot limit you will probably pass your pair of aces.

WARNING: Of the three options, it is often better either to pass or raise. Calling may be the worst choice.

Finally, take (J♣ 4♣) 10♣ A♣ 2♦ against (? ?) 7♠ Q♥ Q♦. You are losing but, at limit, you must keep on calling. At pot limit, you may be a terrible underdog. The right move is to ditch this filth. I have seen players under-raise all-in with the four flush. The queens were certain to call. Now the player hits a blank and the opponent another queen. The player might just as well have torn up the money used to under-raise. There is only one way to describe this play – idiotic.

TIP: Don't waste money due to impatience.

Strategy on Card Six

In limit, if nothing much has changed, simply continue the same way as card five. It is rare to pass, once you have reached this stage. Your opponent has to make what looks like a huge improvement.

An exception might be (Q♦ 7♠) Q♥ 4♦ 9♠ 3♣ against (? ?) 10♦ 8♦ 4♣ K♠. There has been a fair amount of activity. Fifth street you check, he bets and you raise. He calls. Sixth street your opponent comes out betting. Now a pass may be called for. On the other hand it could be a terrible mistake. This is poker, you know!

You have come up against a remarkable opponent if he was bluffing. Let him win. He deserves it for his colossal nerve.

What about (Q♦ 7♠) Q♥ 4♦ 9♠ 7♣ against the same holding? Again your opponent comes out betting sixth street. In limit it is okay to raise or just to call. You are not passing and, if he is bluffing, let him hang himself. He is not about to pass a raise sixth street.

In pot limit it is not a bad idea to raise all-in. Then you have no more problems and no more pain. A strong opponent may pass (K♥ 10♣) 10♦ 8♦ 4♣ K♠ or (K♦ 3♦) 10♦ 8♦ 4♣ K♠. We will be delighted in both cases. He has 21 cards to beat queens up with the latter hand.

This explosion point where there is just one bet left is common at pot limit. Raising all-in certainly simplifies things. However, you may have stopped your opponent bluffing.

TIP: Raising all-in may be the best move, especially if you do not know where you stand.

Many players think, having called on sixth street, that they must call at pot limit on the river. You are supposed to be a poker player, not a computer. You may wish to change your mind.

Drawing Hands

a) Trips

(7♥ 7♦) A♦ 4♦ 7♣ Q♠ against (? ?) 9♣ 4♣ Q♣ 2♣. You have seen four passed cards, none matching any of your 7, A, 4 or Q.

Your opponent looks for all the world like a flush. Even if he does not have it yet, he may hit it on the river. There is no problem at limit. You must call to try to make a full house. Even with two pair you probably have better than 10/1 odds at this stage.

What about pot limit? The pot is $100 and he bets $100. Should you call? You can see 10 cards and four others were passed. Thus there are 38 cards left. You have nine improving cards (outs): one seven, three aces, three fours, and two queens. Thus your odds are $(38{-}9)/9 =$

3.2/1. You are only receiving 2/1 for your money.

If it is all-in, you should pass. Consider if there is still at least $300 left to bet on the river. Now you have the implied odds that he may call if you make your full house. Alternatively, you can check and he will probably bet for you. Now you may win $100+$100+$300 = $500. $100 is a fine sum to pay for such an opportunity.

Get real. He may not have the flush and pass. He may have the flush and pass, especially if you never bluff. If you check, he may check right back, being afraid of your trapping. Alternatively, he may have trip queens or nines and also improve.

In practice this is a marginal call.

b) Flush draw

(9♣ 7♣) 4♣ Q♣ 2♦ J♦ against **Joe** with (? ?) 9♥ 8♣ K♦ 7♠ and **Ali** (? ?) A♦ 5♥ 3♠ 10♦. You have seen four passed cards including one club. Ali has bet to fifth street and checks sixth street. Joe bets and Ali calls. What should you do?

You can see 14 cards and have seen four more = 18. There are seven clubs left. Thus you have not seen 52–18 = 34 cards. Thus your odds are (34–7)/7, i.e. about 4/1.

Once again in limit there is no problem. It is certain you have the odds.

In pot limit, the pot is $100. Joe has bet $100 and Ali called. Thus you have 3/1. That is not enough if it is all-in. To justify calling, you need the implied odds should you manage to improve.

Comes the river and Ali checks. Your last card is 3♣. You bet $250. Joe calls and now Ali raises $1000. What is going on and what should you do?

The answer is, you do not know and neither do I. You cannot be certain that Ali knows what he is doing! You are almost certainly beating Joe – if that is any consolation.

Implied odds are not all they are cracked up to be at pot limit.

Strategy on Card Seven

If you think that your opponent(s) is on a draw, it makes little sense to bet. This is similar to Draw poker. The following dialogue often comes up. A player, who is first to speak, bets all-in on the river with two pair. He is now called by somebody who has just made a flush or straight. Now he says, 'Well, I would have had to call anyway.' Just nod sympathetically.

You hold aces, have not improved, and have been betting all the way at limit. Now I am inclined to check on the river. Even one opponent is favourite to beat that after seven cards. However, I have noticed that some strong players continue to bet. They reckon a smaller pair will have to call. They cannot envisage passing and two pair will bet against a check. They would have to call. Few people raise in this situation with two small pair. Thus they believe the cost is the same. I do not see why the small pair must call.

At pot limit I may make an exploratory bet with my aces. The pot is $100 and I bet $25. However, this strategy must be employed only rarely. A good player will otherwise catch on, and simply raise. Of course, if you know this, you can bet the $25 and thus incite a bluff.

At limit, you have called all the way with one pair and now made two. Whether your only opponent checks or bets, you must raise. Otherwise what were you doing, making all those calls?

At pot limit, low two pair is seldom worth a bet. You are only going to be called if losing.

Trips may well be worth a bet, even at pot limit. Much depends on the shape of your opponent's hand.

TIP: Seven Stud pot limit is often a matter of what you imagine your opponent holds. Your own hand is of less importance.

Sometimes I have felt certain that my opponent had a four flush. Then I have bet out on card five, six and seven with just one ace and no pair. I had to bet on the river with no pair. He may have accidentally made a weak hand and outdrawn me. I had to ensure that there was still money left with which to attack his stack. It was just unlucky if he made his flush. I must admit that I was more likely to play like that 30 years ago! You can play this way at limit as well, but you need a solid, cautious opponent.

If you have called to improve and do so, then you should bet on the river. If you are afraid of being beaten at pot limit, then you should have passed earlier.

Sometimes you are first to speak and hit an absolute monster on the river. For example: (Q♦ J♦) 9♦ K♥ 8♦ 4♣ and your boat comes in with 10♦ on the river. The pot is $100. It is often best to bet out when this happens. It is true that everybody may pass. Also you have discouraged a bluff. Sometimes you will be raised $300. Now you can re-raise $900 and will probably be called. If you check-raise, your opponent is more likely to stop, think and just call, or even pass! A $2700 pot may shrink to $300. This is even true at limit. If you bet, you are more likely to win three bets.

TIP: When holding a monster you may win more by betting than trap-checking.

Playing a Short-Stack at Pot Limit

Sometimes card five or earlier, you may be short of money. The pot is multi-way action and you have a reasonable holding. The pot is $100 and there is a bet before you of $100. There are callers and you can raise all-in for $100. This is mathematically sound. You are going to get good odds for your money. If players pass, you have fewer to beat. If they all call then, on the next card, some may be blasted out by a player. Thus you are likely to be left isolated trying to beat the best hand.

Seven Card Stud is a lifetime study. When you come across unfamiliar nuances, you will be on your way to mastery. Judging the playing strength of your opponents accurately is very important. Ultimately this can be more vital than a short-term run of good cards.

Try It Yourself

Each question should be answered for: a) limit; and b) pot limit.

1. You hold (9♣ 6♣) 7♣. Two clubs are showing and one five.

What should you do: a) facing a bet; b) facing a bet and raise?

2. You hold (10♠ 8♣) 9♣ 7♠.

What should you do: a) facing a check; b) facing a bet with two players with two flushes to follow?

3. You hold (A♣ 9♠) A♦ 4♣ 6♦ against (? ?) 7♠ Q♠ 4♦.

You have bet third and fourth street and been called. Now you bet fifth street and are raised? What should you do?

4. You hold (Q♣ 9♣) 6♣ 9♦ 2♣ Q♠ against (? ?) J♠ 8♣ 2♠ 7♥.

You have called third, fourth and fifth streets. Sixth street you check. He bets. What should you do?

5. You hold (K♠ 3♦ 3♣) K♥ 9♦ 3♠ 4♥ against (? ? ?) J♦ 5♦ A♥ 5♠.

Card three and four you bet. Card five he checks and you bet. Card six he bets and you call. On the river he bets, you raise and he re-raises. What should you do?

Answers on Page 153.

Chapter Five

Omaha Poker

- ♣ Rules of Omaha Poker

- ♣ Holdings before the Flop

- ♣ Looking at the Flop

- ♣ Outs

- ♣ Limit Omaha

- ♣ Five and Six Card Omaha

- ♣ Try it Yourself

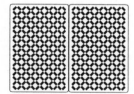 

Rules of Omaha Poker

- Each player receives four cards face down. There is a betting interval.

- There are burn cards as in Hold 'Em.

- Three communal cards are dealt face up in the middle (the flop). There is a betting interval.

- A fourth communal card is dealt face up in the middle (the turn). There is a betting interval.

- A fifth and final card is dealt face up in the middle (the river). There is a final betting interval, after which the cards of each player are shown.

- The player with the best five cards wins, selecting **two** cards from his hand and **three** from the table. Use of less than two from the hand or more than three from the table is not allowed.

- Thus this game is somewhat similar to Hold 'Em.

Your first job is to play out hands for a couple of hours. Learn to recognise the best possible made hand on the flop and also the best drawing hand. Then do the same on the turn and finally the best hand on the river. Continue practising this while playing, even when not in the pot. Eventually this should become second nature to you. Until you have reached this stage, you should only play for very small stakes. Omaha is a complex game and I would hate you to lose money by making a mistake. I can assure you that everybody has made them, including me.

Example 1: Limit

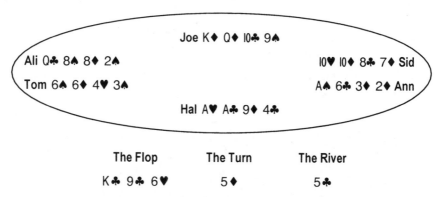

Joe K♦ Q♦ 10♣ 9♠

Ali Q♣ 8♠ 8♦ 2♠   10♥ 10♦ 8♣ 7♦ Sid

Tom 6♠ 6♦ 4♥ 3♠   A♠ 6♣ 3♦ 2♦ Ann

Hal A♥ A♣ 9♦ 4♣

The Flop	The Turn	The River
K♣ 9♣ 6♥	5♦	5♣

Each player antes $5. Tom is first to speak and bets $10. Ali passes. Joe raises $10. Sid calls for $20. Ann passes. Hal raises to $30. Tom, Joe and Sid all call. The pot is $150.

The Flop: K♣ 9♣ 6♥

Tom with trip sixes bets $10. Joe with kings and nines raises $10. Sid can make a straight with a 10, 8, 7, or 5. He calls. Hal can make the nut club flush, trip aces or aces up. He calls. Tom raises, making it $30 to go. All the players call. The pot is $270.

The Turn: K♣ 9♣ 6♥ 5♦

Tom checks. Joe checks. Sid bets $20 and all three players call. The pot is $350.

The River: K♣ 9♣ 6♥ 5♦ 5♣

Tom bets $20. Joe passes. Sid passes. Hal calls. Tom's hand is 6♠ 6♦ 6♥ 5♦ 5♣ a full house. Hal's hand is A♣ 4♣ K♣ 9♣ 5♣ the nut flush. Thus Tom wins a $390 pot.

Before the flop both Ann and Ali had extremely poorly co-ordinated cards. Wisely, they passed. The flop was good for all four players – which is very rare. Tom made the running but it was difficult for him to improve, since Joe blocks his buying a king or nine. But still, he would win the pot if it stopped there. Since the game was limit poker, everyone has far too good odds to consider passing.

Sid makes the best hand on the turn. He is the only person who can have a straight. Everybody must call, even though they guess they are losing, because of the pot odds.

An open pair came on the river. Tom bets. Joe passes. Sid makes a good lay-down. He still has a straight, but reckons he is beaten, probably by a full house, but possibly also by a flush. Hal makes a crying call. He thinks he is losing, but for $20 it is worth a chance, since Tom may be bluffing.

Example 2: Pot limit

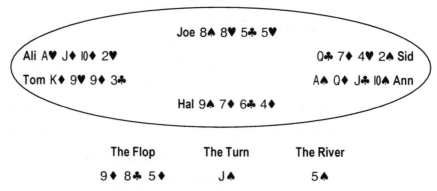

Each player antes $1. Ali is first to speak and opens for $2. Joe calls. Sid passes. Ann calls $2 and raises $12. Hal calls. Tom passes. Ali and Joe call. The pot is $62.

The Flop: 9♦ 8♣ 5♦

Ali's best hand is J♦ 10♦. He can make a flush or straight. He holds six nut outs. He checks. Joe's best hand is trip eights. He also happens to have trip fives. He holds just two nut outs, but may be winning. He checks. Ann's best hand is Q♦ J♣ 10♠. She can make a straight with any queen, jack, ten or seven. She has a wrap-around. J♦, 10♦ or 7♦ may leave her losing to a flush. She has 10 nut outs. She checks. Hal's best hand is 7♦ 6♣, the straight. He bets $60. Ali, Joe and Ann all call. The pot is $302.

The Turn: 9♦ 8♣ 5♦ J♠

Ali's best hand is A♥ J♦ or J♦ 10♦ to make a flush or straight. He checks. Joe's best hand is trip eights. He checks. Ann's best hand is Q♦ 10♠ 9♦ 8♣ J♠. She bets $250. Hal's best hand is 7♦ 6♣, the third best possible straight. He passes, as does Ali. Joe calls. The pot is $802.

The River: 9♦ 8♣ 5♦ J♠ 5♠

Joe's best hand is 5♥ 5♣ 5♦ J♠ 5♠. He bets $600. Ann's best hand is Q♣ 10♠ 9♦ 8♣ J♠. She passes. Joe wins an $802 pot.

Sid and Tom were sensible to pass before the flop. It is true that Tom has a pair of nines but, by itself, that is a mediocre hand at Omaha.

The flop gives all four players something. Again, this unusual, but it has been arranged to show the point. Ali, Joe and Ann can all make hands, but none has anything really good.

When Ann made her hand, it was correct for everybody to fold. Joe has only eight cards with which to make a full house or four of a kind. He is 4/1 against making his hand. The full houses may not even win. In pot limit it was a terrible play for him to call.

However, Joe makes the maximum improvement on the river. His implied odds were not up to much. Ann passed anyway.

Example 3: Limit

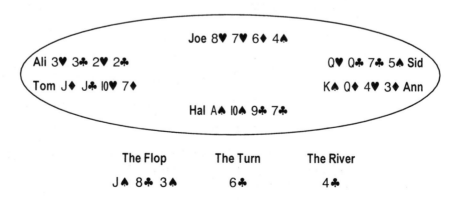

Joe 8♥ 7♥ 6♦ 4♠

Ali 3♥ 3♣ 2♥ 2♣   Q♥ Q♣ 7♣ 5♠ Sid

Tom J♦ J♣ 10♥ 7♦   K♠ Q♦ 4♥ 3♦ Ann

Hal A♠ 10♠ 9♣ 7♣

The Flop	The Turn	The River
J♠ 8♣ 3♠	6♣	4♣

Joe has the small blind of $10. Sid has the big blind of $20. Ann passes. Hal calls $20 and raises $20. Tom raises $20. Ali, Joe, Sid and Hal all call. The pot is $300.

The Flop: J♠ 8♣ 3♠

Joe just has a pair of eights. He checks. Sid has not improved his pair of queens. He checks. Hal can make the nut flush and four different straights. He has a wrap-around. He bets $20. Tom has trip jacks and can make a jack high straight. He raises $20. Ali has trip threes. He calls. Joe and Sid pass. Hal raises $20. Tom makes the third raise of $20. Ali and Hal call. The pot is $540.

The Turn: J♠ 8♣ 3♠ 6♣

Hal can make the nut spade flush, the backdoor club flush and now five different straights. He has a very impressive wrap. Assume that he will lose if it comes an open pair. Then he wins with the A♣, K♠, K♣, any queen or five, any of the remaining tens, nines or sevens, 4♠, 4♣, 2♠, 2♣. He has 24 outs. This is more than half the deck – a great rarity. He bets $40. Tom has the nuts. He raises $40. Ali has trip threes and a backdoor club flush draw. He calls. Hal raises $40 and Tom caps the raises with $40. Ali and Hal call. The pot is $1020.

The River: J♠ 8♣ 3♠ 6♣ 4♣

Hal has made 9♣ 7♣ 8♣ 6♣ 4♣. He bets $40. Tom has J♦ J♣ J♠ 8♣ 6♣. He calls. Ali has 3♣ 2♣ 8♣ 6♣ 4♣. He raises $40. Hal calls. Tom passes. Hal wins a pot of $1220.

Five players all have reasonable hands before the flop. I would not have raised with Tom's holding, but people play in many different ways.

The flop has improved three players. Ali has the usual problem with low trips. He may be winning, or be drawing dead to the case three. Hal has an excellent drawing hand. Tom can see that he has the best made hand at the moment and naturally wants to protect this hand by raising at every opportunity.

Tom's trip jacks are still best on the turn. Hal has improved as a five will now make him a straight. He can also make two different flushes, although the clubs may not be good. Ali does not know whether he is coming or going. For all he knows, his clubs may be winning.

On the river Hal has made a moderate flush and bets. Tom has a terrible foreboding that it has all gone wrong. He makes a crying call. Now Ali raises. This is bad play. One of the other two must surely also have made a club flush. Hal calls gloomily. It is only $40 to Tom and he could win $1220. However, he realises that the game is up. Despite having 30/1 odds, he makes a big lay-down and passes.

If you turn over all three hands on the turn, 16 cards are open to view, leaving 36 unseen. Hal would win with 17 of these and split the pot with 9♥, 9♦. Tom wins with 16 cards and splits the pot with 2. Ali has only one out, 3♦. He is in terrible shape.

Holdings before the Flop

Omaha is unlike most other poker games in that there is no 'best' hand before the flop. You can only hold a 'good' hand. Ideally you would like everybody to pass so that you win the antes uncontested. This happens about once a night in a tight game. Since so many players can hold good hands, there is a great deal of action. It is no use waiting for the nuts. It is not unusual to call the initial bet in 50% of the hands before the flop.

Ideally you would like to hold four cards which are all working together. Examples include:

8♣ 7♦ 6♣ 5♦. You can make a straight with J 10 9, 10 9 8, 10 9 7, 10 9 6, 9 8 7, 9 8 6, 9 8 5, 9 7 6, 9 7 5, 9 6 5, 8 7 4, 8 6 4, 8 5 4, 7 6 4, 7 5 4, 6 5 4, 5 4 3 and 4 3 2. That is 18 different straights, by comparison with four at best for Hold 'Em. You may also make a club or diamond flush with this hand. This is quite apart from four of a kind, full houses, trips, two pair or one pair.

J♠ J♦ 9♠ 9♥. You can make two different trips and several different straights, provided a ten comes. A spade flush is also possible.

K♥ K♦ Q♥ J♠. You can make trip kings, several different straights and a heart flush.

A♦ K♥ Q♦ 10♥. You can make 10 different straights provided a jack comes and two different flushes. Also your pairs and trips may be attractive.

A♠ A♣ K♠ K♣. You know that you are winning before the flop, but can only make one straight. Two nut flushes beckon. It is 50,000/1 against being dealt this hand.

A♥ A♦ J♦ 10♥. Again you are winning before the flop. Now you can make six straights in addition to two nut flushes.

However, if you sit around and wait for these hands, you will wilt away because of the antes.

Elaborate tables exist showing the relative value of hands before the flop. They are totally irrelevant for limit and only useful for all-in coups at pot limit. You need only know this against one opponent. If you have a premium hand, you will not be worse than a 7/4 underdog before the flop.

Three-handed it could become different due to the interaction. I dream of holding: A♠ A♦ 6♠ 5♦ against two opponents, one with K♠ K♣ 8♠ 8♥ and the other K♥ K♦ 8♦ 8♣. They are both drawing totally dead, but would be justified in going all-in.

T.J.'s Theorem

T.J. Cloutier and Tom McEvoy's wrote an otherwise excellent book *Championship Omaha*. In it they recommend that you never make the first raise before the flop at pot limit. It is impossible to knock anyone out who has a playable hand. You are shopping the business on your hand. You should only re-raise. In particular the first raise with aces before the flop is a no-no. To give a clue about half your hand when there are still many bets to come is foolish. I have even sat at the table with T.J. and heard him expound this philosophy.

If you were to raise only with aces, then indeed such action would be nonsense. There is nothing wrong with raising with *any* premium hand. Anybody who then calls with a mediocre hand will eventually be punished.. Admittedly it may take several years for the odds to run true. The problem with re-raising is that you may be escalating the pot into an all-in situation. All your skill in reading the hands after the flop will then have flown out of the window.

Consider 9♥ 8♠ 7♥ 5♦ against A♠ A♦ J♠ 3♦. The former often wins because of the cards that come on the turn and river. For example, with a final board of Q♦ 6♥ 2♦ 3♣ 4♠, 7♥ 5♦ is the best hand. However, the 9 8 7 5 would never consider calling a bet on the flop or the turn. The 9 8 7 5 has made a backdoor straight.

Thus, if you have aces before the flop, the following is a good strategy. Arrange your financial holding so that you can go all-in on the flop. Thus the pot is $100 and you bet $100. The 9 8 7 5 calls. Comes the flop, the pot is now $300 and you have $200 left. Bet it and he will run away.

The 9 8 7 5 can thwart you here. He can re-raise $200 before the flop, knowing that he is losing. Now he has maximised his chance of outdrawing you.

TIP: Going all-in with two or more cards to come maximises your probability of winning with a drawing hand. It also maximises the probability of losing all your money.

Danglers

T.J. places great emphasis on not playing with 'danglers'. For example, with Q♠ J♦ 10♠ 4♥, the 4♥ is a dangler. It has no relevance whatsoever to your other three cards. It can only be valuable with a flop such as 4♦ 4♣ 2♠. A flop of Q♥ 7♠ 4♦ may leave you gasping for breath with no real hope of winning the pot against Q♣ 7♣.

A hand such as Q♠ J♦ 10♠ 4♦ is not fully dangling, as you have two flush draws. However, you are still courting disaster if you cold call a raise here. A♠ Q♦ 10♠ 4♣ is not a full dangle either, as the A 4 may make a straight. TJ does not expound on the virtues of such hands as

K♦ 9♣ 8♠ 7♣. However, we recently discussed this and had independently coined a phrase. The K♦ is a 'reverse' dangler. Clearly this hand is somewhat better than 9♣ 8♠ 7♣ 3♦.

Your attitude must depend on the type of game in which you are playing. If it is loose, you may lose much of your money waiting for a four card hand. Then the flop hits you and you find yourself all-in with a terrific hand – but lose.

Looking at the Flop

Please take a good, long look. Omaha is complex and it is easy to make an error. Decide whether you want to pour money into this pot, just take a stab at it, or pass. Meanwhile, you must also be observing the reactions of your potential opponents. Naturally, this is much easier to do if you are in late position. Poker is usually played very fast. If you only make your decision when it reaches you, then all eyes will be on your reaction. You think you are a smoothie, giving nothing away? Stop kidding yourself! All players sometimes display a response. You do not want your reactions to undergo close scrutiny.

Example 1

Holding A♥ A♠ 9♦ 3♠.

Flop Q♦ J♥ 4♥. Bet in any two- or three- or possibly even four-handed coup, from any position. You may be winning and, if a heart comes, you can try betting with the bare A♥. You will have the blockers if a king or ten comes. If somebody raises you, it will be best to pass. An ace will not give you the nuts, since your opponent may make a straight.

Flop Q♦ J♠ 7♠. Things are looking up. Now you have aces and the nut flush draw.

Flop Q♠ 5♦ 2♠. Not bad. You hold aces, the nut flush draw and a four will make you a straight. The problem is, neither trip aces nor the straight will be the nuts.

Flop A♣ Q♠ 4♠. Your main worry here is persuading anybody to put in any money. You have the nut trips and the nut flush draw. Beware, any king, jack, ten, five, three or two other than spades may give you the losing hand. What is more, in pot limit, you are going to go off in a big way. It is very difficult to reach a totally safe haven in Omaha. Thus slow-playing your hands and giving free cards, is treacherous.

 WARNING: Trapping by slow-play in Omaha is dangerous.

Example 2

Holding A♥ Q♥ J♠ 9♠.

Flop K♥ 10♠ 8♥. This holds a special place in the hearts of all poker players. You will have the nuts with any heart except 10♥ and also an ace, queen, jack, nine or seven. This comes to 21 cards. Feel free to go all-in with such a holding. Promise me though, that you are not playing with all your worldly goods at stake. You are only 3/1 favourite to make your hand and would still lose to a full house if an open pair comes.

Flop 10♦ 8♠ 5♠. Not bad. You can make a straight with queen, jack, nine or seven and can also make a spade flush. Please calculate your number of nut outs. The answer is Q♦, Q♣, J♥, J♦, J♣, 9♥, 9♦, 9♣, 7♥, 7♦, 7♣. This comes to 11. You can put in a great deal of action against one opponent. However, against two or more, one may have the nut flush draw and the other trips.

Flop 10♠ 8♠ 7♣. Do not hold your breath waiting for this holding. You have the nut straight, going higher (with a jack or nine) and can make a straight flush. I like to bet this hand. My opponent(s) may hold the same straight and have virtually no chance of improving. An opponent may hold 10♥ 10♣ and, when the 7♠ comes, be destroyed by the straight flush.

Flop K♦ Q♦ 10♣. You hold the nuts and should be betting. However, your hand is going nowhere. Basically you want people to pass, or for the turn and river to produce blanks.

Flop K♦ 10♦ 9♣. Again you hold the nuts. Now at least you can make a higher straight with a queen or jack. Watch out for those diamonds or pairs!

Flop 9♥ 9♣ 8♦. You may well be winning with A♥ 9♠. Even if you are losing to 8 8 or 9 8, you can still win with an ace, queen or jack. Against A♦ 9♦ 7♠ 7♣, you are splitting the pot, but will win with a queen or jack. Even a ten wins, provided no seven comes.

Example 3

Holding 9♠ 9♦ 7♥ 6♦.

Flop 10♦ 7♦ 6♥. You hold the bottom two pair, a straight flush draw and the blockers. That is to say, it is difficult for anyone to have the straight due to your pair of nines. This is worth a bet if nobody else has taken action. It may even be worth a raise if you are a real daredevil. It is not much of a hand on which to call.

Flop 8♦ 5♣ 2♦. You can improve with a nine, seven, six, four or a diamond. All the straights are the nuts. Thus you have 10 nut outs and the 9♥ or 9♣ will offer you not only the nut straight, but also the nut trips. Your diamond flush draw may be useful.

Outs

Outs are cards which improve your hand, when you may not be winning on the flop. Where they are almost certain to improve your hand, they are referred to as 'nut outs'. Killer cards are the stone-cold nuts. If these turn up, your opponent can now only win the pot with four of a kind.

Please work your way through the next list. It will help you familiarise yourself with this complex game. There is no need whatsoever to commit such lists to memory, but it is essential to be able to recognise at a glance how many outs you have. If you make a mistake by one or two, no harm will be done.

Flop J♠ 9♦ 3♠.

No.	Holding	Outs	Nut Outs	Killer Nut Outs
1.	A♠ K♣ Q♠ 10♥	20	19	none
2.	A♠ A♥ Q♠ 10♥	17	16	2
3.	K♠ Q♣ 10♠ 10♥	19	11	none
4.	K♥ Q♠ 10♥ 8♠	20	10	none
5.	Q♠ J♦ 10♥ 9♠	21	8	2
6.	A♠ 10♥ 8♠ 3♣	15	11	none
7.	10♥ 8♠ 7♣ 6♠	18	2	none
8.	A♠ K♥ 10♦ 9♠	12	12	none
9.	K♠ 10♠ 3♦ 3♣	18	5	1
10.	J♥ J♣ 8♦ 7♣	see below*		1

* You are winning and thus entitled to stake all the money you currently have on the table. Seven cards give you the nut full house, but be careful. *Only* the J♦ is absolutely safe. Any nine or three may give your opponent four of a kind.

Example no. 1 is the best drawing hand. The 9♠ is given as an out. However, what is your opponent playing with? One of his most natural hands is J 9. The 9♠ gives you the nut flush, but your opponent may have a full house.

Thus I tend only to think in terms of the number of nut outs I have. Also I imagine myself to be up against the nut trips.

 TIP: In Omaha concentrate on your nut outs.

Example 2 is not quite as good as the first hand, but it has two special features. Either of the two aces will give you an absolute monster. Also, you may be winning with the pair of aces. Example 1 is the better drawing hand, but it is unlikely that you currently hold the winning hand. With example 2, if a three comes this gives you aces up, which may be winning.

Example 3 is a good hand. Yet you would be in a sorry state if up against one opponent with trips and another with the nut flush draw.

Example 4 is only slightly weaker, but there are now both the ace and king flushes to beat ours.

Example 5 is a premium hand. You may even be winning. Often it is best to go all-in on the flop with such a hand. You do not know in what ways your hand is best.

Example 6 is yet another case of a good hand which can come unstuck.

Example 7 could be a disaster. Yet, if you are up against trips jacks only, you are favourite.

Example 8 is another attractive hand. It is not indicated above, but an ace or king may give you the winning two pair.

Example 9 could be strong or desperately weak. Two handed it must be strong. In multi-way action pots someone may have J J and an opponent the nut flush draw.

Example 10 is normally going to be as good as it gets all week. Don't cry when you get beaten by the nut flush draw. Your opponent may heap money into the pot with virtually no chance – and then win on the river. Just try to grin and bear it.

Number of Outs; Odds against making your Hand

This assumes that you are up against the nut trips. It also assumes you have solely seen those two cards, the flop and your own four. In limit this is almost totally irrelevant as you will have your odds, except at the lowest levels. The odds have been approximated. Samples are shown for important hands.

See table on next page.

You need 17 nut outs to be sure it is a good move to plough in all your money on the flop. You need 11 outs to justify calling an all-in pot bet on the flop. If your opponent can bet and then bet again on the turn, you need 14 outs to stand the heat. Then you can call on the turn as you will be only 2/1 against. These odds do not take into account potential implied odds.

No. of outs	Holding	Flop	2 Cards to come	1 Card to come
4	A♠ Q♠ 10♦ 4♥	J♣ 8♦ 3♥	7/1	9/1
5			6/1	7/1
6			9/2	6/1
7			4/1	5/1
8	A♠ Q♠ 10♦ 4♥	J♣ 9♦ 3♥	3/1	4/1*
8	A♠ Q♠ 10♦ 4♥	J♠ 7♦ 3♠	3/1	5/1*
9	A♠ Q♠ 10♦ 4♥	Q♥ 7♠ 3♠	3/1	4/1
9	A♠ 10♦ 9♠ 8♥	J♣ 7♦ 3♥	5/2	4/1
10			5/2	3.2/1
11			2/1	3/1
12			2/1	5/2
13	A♠ Q♠ 10♦ 4♥	K♣ J♦ 3♥	3/2	9/4
13	A♠ Q♠ J♥ 10♦	9♦ 8♣ 3♥	3/2	9/4
14			3/2	2/1
15			6/5	2/1
16	A♠ K♥ Q♠ 9♦	J♣ 10♦ 3♥	11/10	3/2
17	A♠ J♥ 9♠ 7♣	10♦ 8♣ 3♥	10/11#	3/2
18			4/5	4/3
19			3/4	6/5
20	K♠ Q♠ 9♦ 8♥	J♣ 10♦ 3♥	2/3	11/10
21	A♠ Q♠ J♥ 9♦	K♠ 10♦ 8♠	3/5	evens
22			1/2	9/10
23			1/2	4/5
24			2/5	3/4
25			-	2/3
26			-	3/5

* It seems counter-intuitive that it is easier to make a straight than a flush. With our standard holding A♠ Q♠ 10♦ 4♥, we have eight outs when the flop is J♠ 7♦ 3♠. The turn brings 2♥. Now, when we hit 2♠ on the river, our opponent has made a full house. Thus we are reduced to seven nut outs. Thus indeed it is easier to make a *winning* straight.

\# All odds shown as fractions. Those less than one, mean that you are favourite to win.

With one card to come, your best drawing hand is:

The Turn: J♥ 10♠ 3♠ 2♥. You hold K♥ Q♠ 9♥ 8♠.

Thus you make a straight or flush with aces (4), kings (3), queens (3), nines (3), eights (3), sevens (4), six, five and four of hearts and also spades. This comes to 26 cards. However, you hold only nine nut outs.

If instead you hold A♥ A♠ K♠ Q♥, then you have 22 nut outs with 42 cards unseen (remember that you are assuming your opponent holds J J). This is then slight favourite over trips.

Since Omaha is a game of nuts, it is very useful to hold an ace flush draw in your hand. However, it is not worth calling a raise with a holding such as A♥ 10♠ 7♥ 3♣. The only cards fully working together are the A♥ 7♥. A holding such as A♥ Q♣ 10♠ 7♥ is more promising as you can also make several straights.

Wrap

Whenever you have more than eight cards to make a straight, you are said to have a wrap. As we have seen, it is possible to flop as many as 20 cards to give you a straight.

Backdoor

One reason that Omaha is a baffling game is that it is possible to hit additional possibilities on the turn. For example:

Holding	Flop	Outs	Turn	Outs
A♠ Q♠ 10♦ 4♥	J♠ 7♦ 3♠	8	J♠ 7♦ 3♠ 2♥	10
A♠ Q♠ 10♦ 4♥	J♠ 7♦ 3♠	8	J♠ 7♦ 3♠ 9♥	13
A♠ Q♠ 10♦ 4♦	J♠ 7♦ 3♠	8	J♠ 7♦ 3♠ 2♦	14
A♠ Q♠ 10♦ 9♦	J♠ 7♦ 3♠	11	J♠ 7♦ 3♠ K♦	24

The backdoor flush in the last two examples is the most important. Holding this potential adds 3% to the probability of your winning. A 3/1 shot has become 5/2 with two cards to come. The fact that the second flush is not the nuts is less important now. You cannot run scared from every phantom possibility. You can even hold two backdoor flushes. This adds 6% in all. That 3/1 shot has become 9/4.

Drawing to beat a Made Straight

Number of outs	Holding	Flop	2 Cards to come	1 Card to come
4	A♠ Q♠ 10♦ 4♥	Q♣ 10♥ 8♣	9/2	9/1
7, then 10*	Q♠ Q♥ 2♠ 2♦	Q♣ 10♥ 8♣	9/5	3.2/1
10, then 13*	K♣ Q♠ Q♥ 10♦	Q♣ 9♠ 8♣	11/10	7/3
15, then 17*	A♠ Q♠ Q♥ 2♦	Q♣ 9♠ 8♠	2/3#	3/2

*When playing to make a full house from trips, there are three extra pairing cards on the turn. This is due to the chance of pairing the new card.

#Once again, this means that you are favourite to make this hand.

Duplication

It is quite normal for your opponent to hold part of your hand. Also, it is dangerous to make assumptions about what your opponents hold.

Holding	Opponent Holding	Flop	Number of outs left
A♠ Q♠ 10♦ 4♥	Q♥ Q♦ J♠ 9♥	Q♣ 10♥ 8♣	0
A♠ Q♠ 10♦ 4♥	J♠ 10♦ 10♣ 9♥	Q♣ 10♥ 8♣	2
A♠ Q♠ Q♥ 2♦	J♠ 9♣ 8♥ 8♦	Q♣ 10♥ 8♣	4, then 7 on turn
A♠ Q♠ Q♥ 2♦	Q♥ J♠ 9♠ 8♣	Q♣ 10♠ 8♠	11, then 13 on turn

The better co-ordinated your hand, the less easy your opponent will find it to outdraw you.

Aces against Aces

If you have aces and find yourself in a raising war, it is quite likely that he, too, has aces.

In limit there will come a point where there is no purpose in a further raise.

In pot limit, if you are first to speak, he has a positional advantage. You can take this away from him by going all-in before the flop. Alternatively you can call and then bet out no matter what the flop is. You may bluff him out of a hand that would otherwise split the pot. There is no need to worry that he will outdraw you. He would not have passed when faced with one more raise before the flop. Once he is in such a war, then he will not contemplate passing. If you have dry aces, that are totally ill co-ordinated, you may choose to pass. If you are last to speak, you have an advantage over your opponent. Why would you want to go all-in and thus precipitate a sheer gamble?

If there is more than one opponent, then matching aces are in a poor state of health. A hand such as 10♠ 9♣ 8♦ 6♠ is probably favourite over the two hands.

Both Players on a Draw

I had the following experiences against the same player in the space of just one week. I have made my holding identical in both cases to simplify matters. I held J♠ 10♥ 7♠ 6♦.

In both cases the flop was 9♦ 8♠ 4♥. Glory be! I had hit the magical 20 card wrap. This is very rare, not least because my starting hand is of poor quality. 9 8 must come to give me a good hand. Thus it should be passed before the flop if there is a great deal of action.

In both cases Corky was sitting to my immediate left. The pot was $1000. In the first case, I bet out and he raised the pot. Now I raised $9000 and he called. There was just $2000 left to bet. What am I to make of this? He is probably also on a wrap. He will be prepared to pass if an open pair comes or if he makes nothing.

The next card produced 2♦. No improvement for me, in fact I am threatened by a possible backdoor flush. I checked as did Corky. Last card K♥. Thus the board cards were 9♦ 8♠ 4♥ 2♦ K♥.

I now bet the last $2000 and he passed, showing his drawing hand, lamenting his luck. It was still better than mine, A J 10 7. I did not show my bluff.

The second time around I checked on the flop, Corky bet $1000 and I raised $3000. Once again he just called. The reasoning is similar, he is probably again on a drawing hand.

The turn produced 9♦ 8♠ 4♥ 2♠. Now I can hit a backdoor flush. I bet $7000. Corky called.

The river 9♦ 8♠ 4♥ 2♠ K♥. I bet the last $4000. Corky again passed, showing his A J 10 7, and lamenting his luck. The hand would once again have won.

Twice then I had hit a legendary drawing hand. However, I escaped intact only because I left room to bluff at the river. It is often comforting to have a pair to declare at the end. Inevitably though this means you have fewer outs.

Both Players with Made Straights

Example 1: Flop J♥ 10♠ 9♣.

You hold K♣ Q♠ 9♠ 8♦. You bet on the flop and are raised. If there is only one bet left, you may as well go all-in.

One bad scenario is that he holds A K Q 9. Now he has four cards to make a higher straight, K K and Q Q. This provides a 19% chance that you will lose the pot.

The terrifying possibility is that he holds K Q 10 10. Now he has six chances on the turn and nine on the river of winning by pairing up. This is a 34% probability of his winning the whole pot. If you knew this then you should pass, 33% being the figure where it pays to do so with the nuts.

Example 2: Flop 10♥ 9♠ 8♥.

You hold A♥ Q♣ J♠ 2♦. You bet the flop and are raised. If you re-raise and then bet the turn, you are representing the straight and flush draw. You will probably run out of money to bluff the bare A♥, if a heart should turn up on the river. Discretion is the better part of valour. Call and keep on calling, if no improving card arrives. Sometimes you may prefer to pass. Since you opened the betting, it is harder to bluff a flush. Had you just been a passive caller, then representing the flush draw looks more realistic.

Example 3: Flop J♥ 10♠ 7♣.

You hold K♣ Q♠ 9♠ 8♦. If you are provided the opportunity, go to the table, that is, put in all your money. The best he can muster is J J 9 8. He wins if an open pair falls. If this does not happen, you have five winning cards, any ace, king, queen, nine or eight. He wins the whole pot 36% of the time. You pick it up 44% of the time. The remaining 20% it will be split. If he should have such as J 9 8 6, you are free-rolling. That is, you can win with 14 cards and lose with none. You win it all 57% of the time and can only lose to two running cards, such as 6 J. Life does not come sweeter than this.

Example 4: Flop J♥ 10♠ 7♠.

You hold K♣ Q♠ 9♠ 8♦. This is a fabulous hand, yet you could be up against three players, one with the nut trips, another with the nut flush draw and a third splitting the pot with you. Nobody said Omaha was a certainty.

TIP: If your four cards are co-ordinated, the likelihood of a disaster is sharply diminished.

TIP: There are more improving cards to such as J 10 7, than to J 10 9.

Mediocre Hands

Do not fall into the trap of thinking that life is full of wraps, made hands and nut flushes. It is often much more prosaic.

Example 1: Flop K♦ 7♥ 4♠.

You hold A♥ K♥ 9♠ 3♠ and there are three other players in the pot. You should bet. You may be winning and, if not, an opponent may pass 7 4 or even K 4. If called, an ace may fall. If somebody else bets, pass. Your only hope is that you are splitting the pot or that the bettor holds 6 5.

Example 2: Flop K♦ 7♦ 4♠.

You again hold A♥ K♥ 9♠ 3♠. You should be even more ready to bet this hand. A caller is much more likely to be on a draw than before. If a diamond comes down, switch off. If somebody bets, I may or may not call. If one player bets and another calls, fold gracefully. Only one can have the nut flush draw, the other should have two pair or perhaps even trips.

Bits and Pieces

Example: Flop 8♥ 5♠ 3♥.

You hold 6♣ 5♥ 4♥ 3♠. This is well worth a bet; it may be worth a call. Against two opponents it is extremely ugly. Your only nut outs are 2♠, 2♦, 2♣.

There remains a great deal to Omaha on the turn and river. It takes a long time to realise that deception is entirely possible in this game. That is why this section has mainly been devoted to technique before and after the flop.

Limit Omaha

Little of the above means much in limit Omaha. The problem is that the standard staking structure in Vegas is all wrong. The bet is one unit both before and after the flop and two units on the turn and the river. This is the same as in Hold 'Em and Seven Card Stud, yet this is a nine card game, whereas they are seven cards. It is impossible to protect your hand, as it becomes worthwhile to draw to an inside straight. The game would be better played one unit before the flop, two on the flop, and four on the turn and river. However, poker players are creatures of habit.

It still pays to play for the nuts in limit Omaha. Also you should try to get away from mediocre holdings as quickly as possible. Otherwise you may be sucked into a maelstrom of odds, where you have to keep calling. In some ways you should play tighter before the flop in limit Omaha. Once the flop comes, it is difficult to pass holding mediocre draws.

 TIP: In limit games your initial holding should be stricter than in pot limit.

Five and Six Card Omaha

In this game, instead of four cards everyone receives five or six. The game is played in exactly the same way as four card Omaha. Naturally the possibilities are far greater. You must realise that you are not only looking for the nuts, but also the over nuts. That is, your cards should be threatening to win in at least two ways. It becomes a game virtually solely of technique and has little to do with deception. One thing, though, players will believe the bare ace is the nut flush. It needs four to that suit in their own hand to make them suspicious.

Try It Yourself

Each question should be answered for limit and pot limit.

1) You hold a) J♥ 10♠ 9♣ 7♥; b) A♠ A♥ 9♦ 6♠ and are last in hand. The blinds have bet and a couple of players have called. Should you pass, call or raise?

2) You hold a) A♠ Q♦ J♥ 9♠; b) Q♥ Q♦ 9♦ 8♠ and you have called one raise already. Now there are two more raises before it gets back to you. Should you pass, call or raise?

3) You hold a) K♥ J♦ J♣ 8♠; b) 8♠ 8♦ 7♥ 5♦ and the flop is Q♥ 9♦ 8♣. Two players are in front of you who have checked and one is after you. For each example: i) Should you check or bet? ii) How should you respond to a bet?

4) You hold a) A♠ A♥ K♥ 10♦; b) K♦ 10♠ 9♦ 8♣; c) A♠ A♥ 7♣ 5♥. The flop is A♠ Q♥ J♥. You are first to speak. Should you bet or check?

5) You hold 9♠ 8♥ 7♣ 4♥. The flop was 7♠ 6♥ 2♣ and you called a bet. The turn brought forth 7♠ 6♥ 2♣ 3♥. Again you called a bet. Now the river is 7♠ 6♥ 2♣ 3♥ Q♥. Your opponent again bets. Should you pass, call or raise?

Answers on Page 154.

Chapter Six

Lowball Poker

- ♣ **Razz**

- ♣ **London Lowball**

- ♣ **Deuce to Seven**

- ♣ **Ace to Five**

- ♣ **Try it Yourself**

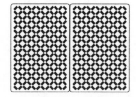

In these versions of poker, the best *low* hand wins. Lowball is often described as the reverse of high poker. This is only partially true. Part of the colour of the game is lost because you are not aiming for straights or flushes. Thus the game is simpler and, in that sense, it is purer poker. As usual, there are many variations of the game.

Razz

Here the best low hand is 5 4 3 2 A, which is called the bicycle or wheel. Neither straights nor flushes count against you. This game is always played limit in Las Vegas, as a version of Seven Card Stud. The high card has to start the betting. From fourth street on, the best low hand showing starts the betting. The betting structure is identical to that explained in Chapter 4.

Example

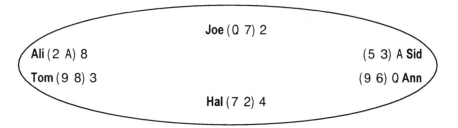

(Note that in this game we do not need specify suits. They are irrelevant.)

Each player antes $1. Ann has to open for $2. Hal calls. Tom calls. Ali calls. Joe calls. Sid raises $2. Ann passes. Hal re-raises $2. Tom passes. Ali calls. Joe passes. Sid makes the third and last raise, capping it. Hal and Ali call. The pot is $34.

Fourth Street

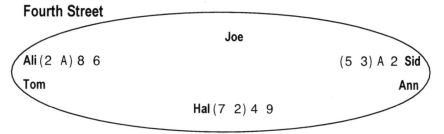

Sid bets $2. Hal calls. Ali raises $2. Sid re-raises $2. Hal calls. Ali calls. The pot is $52.

Fifth Street

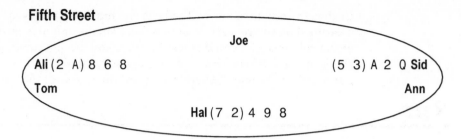

Hal bets $4. Ali calls. Sid raises $4. Hal re-raises $4. Ali and Sid both call. The pot is $88.

Sixth Street

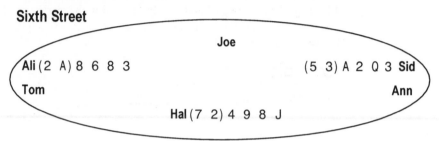

Hal checks. Ali checks. Sid bets $4. Hal passes. Ali calls. The pot is $96.

Seventh Street

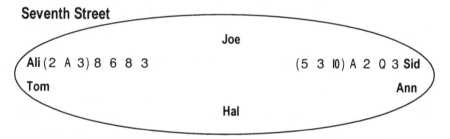

Sid bets $4 and Ali passes. Sid wins a pot of $100.

A brutal aspect of this game is that Ann had to waste $2 betting with a hand that has no hope. They say, 'what goes around, goes around', but I am sure that I am stuck with the high card more often when I am losing than when I am winning!

Tom and Joe should not have wasted $2 each calling with bad hands, but please don't tell them this next time you see them! Note how Hal slow-played his hand initially and then moved in to try to push out the weak hands.

Hal should probably have passed fourth street. Ali tried to lean on him by raising, even though he thought he had the worst of it against Sid. When Hal would not shift for a double raise, Ali gave up trying for the last raise.

Perhaps Hal would do better checking fifth street. Then Sid bets, he raises and Ali may give way under pressure. He must perhaps face putting in $16 to win a pot with $64 in it. As it is, he first faced a bet of $4 to win a pot of $56. When Ali would not shift, Sid did not bother with the last raise.

On sixth street Hal lost interest. He is facing two monsters. Ali checked. After all, it is unlikely that Sid has paired up. Sid bet even though he has indeed paired up.

On seventh street the best that Sid could muster was 10 5 3 2 A. As a last desperate gasp he put in a $4 bluff. Ali is no fool. He has 8 6 3 2 A, but Sid has shown strength throughout and surely cannot have paired when he hit that three? After all, he now has two of them himself.

Ali has made a big lay-down, patting himself on the back for not wasting $4. You, being relatively inexperienced, would not have made this mistake. You would have called for 'value'. So, probably would I. Yet Ali is right, it is about 30/1 against Sid having paired up on the three. Also, even if he did so, he might have improved on the river. Sid, being a gentleman, does not show the bluff.

Ali has fallen into a major poker trap. Calling would have been a small error if Sid had his hand. Passing was a major mistake.

 WARNING: Don't make major errors in order to avoid small ones.

Strategy On Card Three

Basically you want to start with three low cards eight or better. Naturally 3 2 A is best of all. The other consideration is the number of your cards that are out. 3 2 A is not that much of a hand if four other players each have a six showing. Your probability of making a good hand is then severely diminished.

The skill is substantially similar to the other limit games. You want to avoid being sucked in for the ride because each bet is apparently so cheap. (9 7) A is likely to be a losing proposition against two players each showing a low card. With multi-way action, the hand is only slightly superior to (7 A) 9. You are unlikely to bluff anybody out who is under the impression you have stronger hole cards.

Naturally, if the high card jack opens and everybody passes to you, then you will raise even with (K K) 7. He may well pass and, even if he does not, fourth street may show (? ?) J Q against (K K) 7 9. The pot will then be yours for the taking.

You will be dealt three to an eight low about 18% of the time. Thus in an eight-handed game, there should only be an average of two contestants. However, you will observe a higher number of players due to bluffing and loose play.

Strategy on Fourth Street

You hold (7 4) 2 J against (? ?) A 5. He bets. Should you call?

Clearly he has much the better hand if he has not paired up. Let us examine the probabilities. We will assume that the passed cards show average distribution.

You assume that he has two cards below a nine in the hole and that these are not matching. Since you do not have a five, he has paired up 31% of the time. Even if he has done so, then he is still favourite with more betting. This is because you may again hit a bad card and he hit a good one. Then you will have to pass. It is reasonable to assess your chance of winning as about half the time he has paired up. You are likely to win 15% of the time.

Thus you need at least 6/1 odds to call. That is, if it is $2 to you, there must be more than $12 in the pot. Remember this $2 is not the end of it. Suppose that you call and both you and your opponent hit good cards next time. In that case there will be another $4 to call – and so it goes on.

TIP: Pass fourth street if your hand looks like a bust, unless you have better than 6/1 odds.

Holding (7 4) 2 J against (? ?) A 5 we are either a big underdog or small favourite. It is worth reiterating an earlier warning here:

WARNING: Avoid situations where you are either a small favourite or big underdog.

Facing two or more players who overlay your hand, you need very good odds indeed.

Sometimes a third player pulls you in.

You hold (7 4) 2 J. Joe bets his (? ?) A 5. Ann comes in with (? ?) 7 K. Now you know you are beating her, but not by much. Do you trust Ann? If so, she, like you, should not have a five in the hole, which would decrease Joe's likelihood of having paired up.

Had Ann called with (? ?) 7 10, then watch out. You *know* that you are losing to her and beating a ten low is not a certainty. Change Ann's hand to (? ?) 5 10 and there is an additional negative. It is unlikely that Joe has paired on his five.

Strategy on Fifth Street

One important fact should be noted here. If you hold (7 4) 2 6 K against (? ?) 3 8 9, then you are favourite. With two cards to come, you win about 55% of the time. Moreover, he is stuck in the pot forever, whereas you can pass a bust on the river.

TIP: On fifth street hands such as K 7 5 3 2 **are favourite against hands such as** 9 8 6 2 A.

Strategy on Sixth Street

If you know that you are winning, you are almost certainly favourite, no matter how weak your hand.

Strategy on Seventh Street

Do not bet into a hand that is solely drawing and cannot call you, unless he improves. That is, unless you are yourself on a total bluff.

WARNING: Do not bet into a hand that must be on a draw, except as a bluff.

London Lowball

This is also Seven Card Stud and is just like Razz, except that it is played pot limit *and* straights and flushes count for high. The hand (5 4 3) 5 3 2 A looks tremendous, but your lowest hand is 4 3 3 2 A – a pair of 3s. An ace counts low. Thus the royal low is 6 4 3 2 A.

Since it is played pot limit, usually you get only 2/1 odds for your money. However, it is true that the implied odds are far higher. If there are two opponents in the pot, then you will have at least 3/1 for your money. But remember, now you have two players to beat not one.

Note: The more players in the pot, the better the odds, but the more difficult it is to win the pot.

Note that 5 4 is a less attractive-looking hand than 7 2. It may be straightening. By the same token, if it is not then, against a strong opponent, the hand is even stronger.

You hold (7 2) 5 4 3 against (? ?) 2 6 8. Checking here can be extremely effective. You may have paired up or have hit a straight. Your opponent may well bet the pot and he will be exposed to a massive raise. Do, however, remember you cannot make a six low next card. 7 2 5 4 3 6 is no change. 7 2 5 4 3 A is a royal seven. That is 7 4 3 2 A.

On sixth street (7 2) 5 4 Q 4 is about as good as (? ?) A 8 9 J, provided that there is more betting to come on the river. The former hand can make a nine low with 17 cards, eight low with 14 and seven low with 11. Don't take my word for it, add them up. The drawing hand can choose to bet or not on the river. It is very difficult for the 9 8 to pass.

TIP: Made hands should try to go all-in with cards to come against drawing hands. That is, unless the latter is favourite to win.

Deuce to Seven

This is five card draw played no limit. The ace counts high and straights and flushes count against you. Thus the royal low is 7 5 4 3 2.

Example

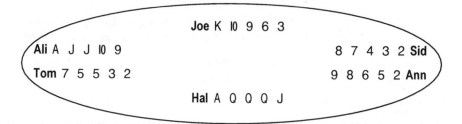

Everybody antes $1. Sid is first to speak and opens for $5. Ann calls $5 and raises $30. Hal passes. Tom calls. Ali and Joe pass. Sid calls $30 and raises $200. Ann passes and Tom calls. The pot is $511.

Sid stands pat (draws no cards). Tom throws away one of his 5s and buys an 8.

Sid holds 8 7 4 3 2. **Tom** holds 8 7 5 3 2.

Sid is still first to speak and he checks. Tom checks back. Sid wins the $511 pot with the better eight low.

It is unusual for there to be three exceptional hands as here. Ann played perfectly correctly to raise, but when Sid re-raised, she did well to pass a rough 9 8. Tom should not have called, although the prospect of making a royal is very enticing.

Sid's check after the draw is virtually automatic. He must leave Tom space to bluff. However, Tom has made a good hand and decided to check it down. He perhaps felt heat coming from Sid suggesting that he was in no mood to pass.

Odds against being dealt Pat Hands

Hand	Odds
7 5 4 3 2	2547/1
7 6 low or better	636/1
8 low or better	141/1
9 low or better	48/1
10 low or better	20/1

Odds on drawing Two Cards

Hand	Odds
Odds on making a 7 low	22/1
Odds on making an 8 low	10/1
Odds on making a 9 low	6/1
Odds on making a 10 low	7/2
Odds on making a J low	9/4
Odds on making a Q low	3/2
Odds on making a K low	11/10

The odds assume that you started with both a seven and a two in your hand, in addition to a three, four or five. Should you start with such as 6 3 2, then buying a four and five is useless.

WARNING: Never call a big bet with the intention of taking two cards. If the bet is small, never call without 7 2 and one of 3, 4 or 5.

Odds on drawing One Card

	Starting with K 7 4 3 2	Starting with K 7 5 4 3
Odds on making a royal	11/1	11/1
Odds on making any 7	5/1	11/1
Odds on making an 8 low or better	3/1	5/1
Odds on making a 9 low or better	2/1	3/1
Odds on making a 10 low or better	4/3	2/1
Odds on making a J low or better	10/11	4/3

It is extremely advantageous to be last to act. If your sole opponent draws two cards, then you can stand pat on J 9 6 3 2 – if you wish.

It is clearly advantageous to go all-in when you have a moderate hand. Take 10 9 8 5 2. You are first to speak and have called a small bet. There is one remaining opponent who raises. Now you can raise all-in. If he calls, then you stand pat. There is little reward to be had from discarding that 10. The best you can make is 9 8 low. If he draws one card, you are favourite. If he stands pat, you will probably have to call for more chips.

Had he been first to act and rapped pat, you could have taken one card and prayed. However, you will look silly if you have thrown away a winner.

If you raise all-in, your opponent can put you on a rough low, trying to buy the pot. Instead, being sneaky, you may have raised all-in with an extremely strong hand.

Using the above table of probabilities, it is poor play to call a re-raise and draw one card.

Occasionally you will raise with rubbish, stand pat and bet out after the draw. This will often secure you the prize.

Often the issue comes down to, 'Does he have it or not?' That is why it is such a pure form of poker.

Ace to Five

This is a draw game. It is played with the bicycle being the best hand, i.e. 5 4 3 2 A is best. Often there is a Joker as the 53rd card, which counts for any card you like. It may be played limit or pot limit.

Clearly it is much easier to get a low hand in this version than at deuce to seven. You will also be receiving better odds for your draw. Your opponent cannot over-bet the pot.

Odds on being dealt Pat Hands

Hand	Odds
5 4 3 2 A	1250/1
6 low or better	500/1
7 low or better	100/1
8 low or better	40/1
9 low or better	18/1

Still, please do not draw two cards even to Joker 2 A. It is 11/2 against making a 7 low. Joker 3 2 A is very strong. The odds against making a seven low or better are only 2/1. Since you hold the joker, it is *significantly* easier for you to improve than anybody else.

In this game you are much more likely to be called if you stand pat. You hold the extraordinarily unlikely Joker A A A. Then the odds against his making a nine low drawing one card are still only 9/5. In addition, you cannot over-bet the pot.

Try It Yourself

1) Seven Stud. You hold (8 4) 10 and were high card. Everybody passes except one player who has raised with (? ?) 7. Should you call or pass in a) Razz; b) London Lowball?

2) Seven Stud. You hold (3 2) 8 5 9. Your one opponent holds (? ?) A 7 Q. What should you do in a) Razz; b) London Lowball?

3) Draw. You hold 7 3 2. You cannot be raised and you have 4/1 odds to call. What should you do in a) Deuce to Seven; b) Ace to Five with a Joker?

4) Draw. You hold 7 6 4 3 2. There has been a bet and raise to you. What should you do in a) Deuce to Seven; b) Ace to Five with a Joker?

5) Draw. You have raised before the flop and stood pat with 8 5 4 3 2. Your one opponent has drawn one card. You are first to speak. What should you do in a) Deuce to Seven; b) Ace to Five with a Joker?

Answers on Page 156.

Chapter Seven

High-Low Poker

- ♣ **Seven Stud High-Low Eight or Better**
- ♣ **Strategy**
- ♣ **Omaha Eight or Better**
- ♣ **Pot Limit**
- ♣ **Try it Yourself**

In these forms of poker, the best high hand splits the pot with the best low hand. I trust that you have read the previous chapters on Seven Stud, Omaha and Lowball. Without basic grounding in those games, you will simply be all at sea here.

There are many ways in which the game of High-Low can be played. We will stick with two forms that are currently popular: Seven Stud eight or better and Omaha eight or better. They are both played limit in America and pot limit in Europe. The same principles apply. Here we shall concentrate on limit High-Low, although a section on pot limit appears towards the end of the chapter.

The very best high hand is a royal flush and the very best low hand is a wheel 5 4 3 2 A. An ace can count high or low.

Note that you cannot have a low hand without at least an eight low. Thus in Seven Stud A A 9 9 4 3 2 loses the high to J J J Q 5 4 2. The first hand gets no part of the low side of the pot as 9 4 3 2 A does not count at all. The required eight low is said to be a qualifier.

You may find yourself involved in a game where there is no cap on the low. Then, in the above example, 9 4 3 2 A is fine for low. The strategy then is always to play for low. Such a hand may also break out into a high, but the reverse can never be true.

Seven Stud High-Low Eight or Better

Example 1

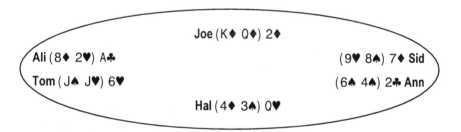

Everybody antes $10. Ann has the low hand as 2♣ ranks below 2♦. She must bet at least $10, with a maximum of $30. She bets $10. Hal passes. Tom raises to $30. Ali calls. Joe calls. Sid calls. Ann raises $30. Everybody calls. The pot is $360.

Fourth Street

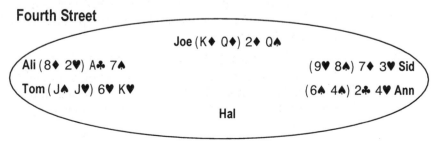

From now on, the high card opens the betting. Ali checks. Joe bets $30. Sid passes. Ann raises $30. Everybody calls. The pot is $600.

Fifth Street

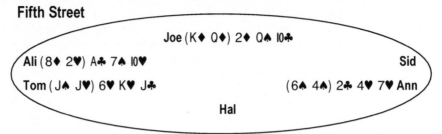

Ali checks. Joe checks. Ann bets $60. Tom raises $60. Ali passes. Joe passes. Ann calls. The pot is $840.

Sixth Street

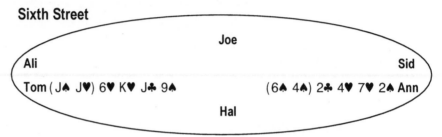

Ann checks. Tom bets $60 and Ann calls. The pot is $960.

Seventh Street

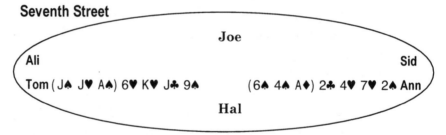

Ann bets $60 and Tom calls. The pot is $1080. Ann's best low is 7♥ 6♠ 4♠ 2♣ A♦. Her high is 4♠ 4♥ 2♣ 2♠ A♦. Tom has no low. His high is J♠ J♥ J♣ A♠ K♥. They split the pot and each receives $540.

Third street Hal correctly threw away his garbage immediately. Tom has a deceptive hand. It looks like a low, but is actually high. Ali has three to a low. The ace is good, but he cannot make a straight or flush. Joe has a quite mediocre hand. However, it is deceptive as he is showing a low card. Sid really should pass. His potential high is weak and he has no real hope of a low.

Fourth street I would have bet with Ali's hand. He played too passively. Had he bet and Joe raised, it is even possible that Ann would have passed! Instead Joe bet, clearly indicating that he is going high. Sid correctly passed. Now Ann made a gutsy raise, indicating a hand that she did not have. This cowed everybody, so they just called.

Fifth street Ann continues her semi-bluff. She has a good draw to a low, but nothing yet. Tom's raise shows that he must have an extremely good hand. After all, he is prepared to tangle with what looks like a made low. It appears that half the pot belongs totally to Ann. Ali and Joe pass. Ann has succeeded in isolating herself with the best hand in a big pot.

Sixth street Ann knows Tom is there to the end. She checks in the hope that Tom will do the same. He knows better and bets out. Obviously Ann must call.

On the river Ann has finally made her low and can bet with impunity. Tom of course calls. Had he made a full house, he would have raised. After all, Ann may turn up with a lower full house. With her lock for low, she could then have re-raised, but it would have been a wasted effort.

The pot is split and each player receives $540. Their actual profit each is $170 each. Yet they each risked $370.

TIP: The prime objective in high-low is to win the whole pot, not just half of it.

Example 2

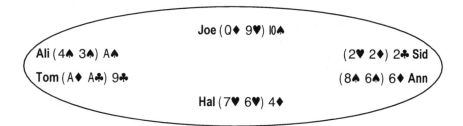

Everybody antes $1. Sid must open the betting, and does so for $1. Ann calls. Hal makes it $2. Tom calls. Ali puts in $4, raising $2. Joe passes. Sid puts in $5, raising $2. Ann, Hal and Tom call. Ali caps the raises with $2 more. Everybody calls. The pot is $46.

Fourth Street

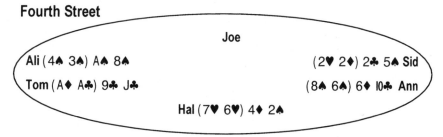

Ali bets $2. Sid raises $2. Ann passes. Hal and Tom call. Ali raises $2. Sid makes the third raise and everybody calls. The pot is $76.

Fifth Street

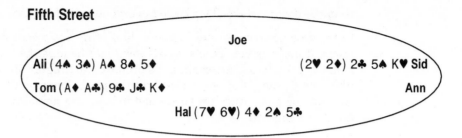

Ali bets \$4. Sid raises \$4. Hal re-raises \$4. Tom passes. Ali and Sid call. The pot is \$112.

Sixth Street

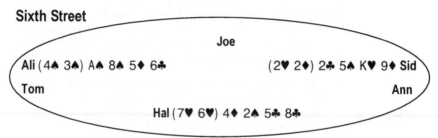

Ali bets \$4. Sid calls. Hal raises \$4. Ali and Sid call. The pot is \$136.

Seventh Street

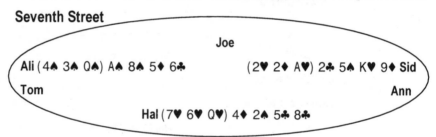

Ali bets \$4. Sid calls. Hal raises \$4. Ali re-raises \$4. Sid calls. Hal raises \$4, capping it once again. Ali and Sid call. The pot is \$184. Sid has lived and died with his wired-up deuces. Hal has an eight high straight and 7 6 5 4 2 low. He also wins nothing. Ali has A♠ Q♠ 8♠ 4♠ 3♠ for high and 6 5 4 3 A for low. He scoops the pot, winning \$127.

On third street Joe must have been pleased that he never had a hand to enter into this pot. Sid's pulse quickened when he started with low trips. These are usually utterly magical at this game. Ann's hand is a bit going both ways. Hal has a good start, it has potential in both directions. You will note that Tom has aces, but never makes a move in the pot. His hand is strictly one way and there is no disguise. The nine up-card (called the door card) is useless for low. Ali is also off to a terrific start. You rarely see so much action in one hand.

On fourth street Ali has a tremendous two-way hand. Sid's is still wonderful, it is extremely deceptive, looking like a low. Ann's hand has run out of steam and she correctly ditches it. Hal knows that he has a fine low draw, but there are many low cards out and he has nothing for high. Tom is still in there; his aces still look good.

On fifth street Ali has made a low and has the makings of a high. Sid still raises, showing to the world that his true strength is probably high. Hal knows that he is winning the low and re-raises. Tom has had enough and discards his aces. Ali and Sid now just call.

On sixth street Ali has made a six low and is feeling pretty good. He bets and there is too much money in the pot for Sid to consider passing. Hal raises. This causes Ali to stop and think. Hal could have him beaten for low. He just calls as does Sid.

Finally, on the river Ali now not only has a six low, but also a flush. Hal cannot see how he can be losing both ways with a straight and seven low. Sid just goes along for the ride, hoping that one of them has gone mad.

Strategy

Starting off with three to a low is all very well, but usually it will break off card four. You expect to make four to a low 40% of the time. Thus you want your hand to go both ways. An ace is always strong; if you pair up that may win the high. Three to a low straight is good and three to a low flush even more enticing. No pair less than pictures should be considered. Remember that the philosophy of 'it's only $2' will result in money trickling through your hands like sand.

It may seem that, because you can hit either a high or low hand, that you should play *more* hands at high-low. This is fallacious. Usually you will win only half a pot. Thus you should play *fewer* hands in this type of game. You should play *tighter*. Hands such as (8♦ 3♣) 6♠ or (10♠ 4♥) 10♦ should often be ditched.

TIP: High-Low should be played tighter than Straight High or Low.

On fourth street broken one-way lows should be ditched. Holding such as (7♥ 5♥) 4♠ Q♦, you do not have the odds to continue if the pot is small. If there was a great deal of action from the off, you will now have to carry on doggedly. It is all your own fault if you got over-excited and put in several raises yourself. Just because your low broke off, does not mean that it is necessarily hopeless. (7♥ 5♥) 4♠ Q♥ can develop both ways. Remembering all the cards passed helps. If several hearts have shown, the hope of a flush is pretty forlorn. (7♥ 5♥) 4♠ 7♠ is not broken off at all. It is a very deceptive hand, which might become extremely rewarding short-handed.

TIP: Keeping track of the passed cards is of enormous importance in Stud Eight or Better.

Fifth street when the limit doubles is usually the moment of truth.

This is just as in Seven Stud. Getting away from mediocre hands is a major part of the skill. Remember that your junk will probably only secure half the pot if it survives to the river. It is entirely possible in our $2-$4 game that the pot at this stage is just $16. If your single opponent bets $4, and you call $4 on 5, 6 and 7, then it is going to cost you $12. This is all just in order to win $8.

Sometimes you will have a low lock against two opponents going high. For example:

(8♠ 3♣) 6♥ 2♦ 7♣ against (? ?) Q♦ 9♠ 7♥ and (? ?) K♠ 10♣ 5♦. The third player bets. It may be best just to call. If you raise, the player with the queen may simply pass. Then you will split a small pot with the high. You need two cards to break into a useful high.

TIP: Holding a lock against two players going the other way can be highly profitable.

With (8♠ 5♣) 6♥ 2♦ 7♣ you may again wish just to call or to raise. You are now trying hard to win the whole pot and perhaps want to thin out the opposition.

If you have a high to start with, you want to thin out the field as much as possible. Ideally you want to be left alone with one low draw which fails to materialise. It is not so easy to make an eight low. You are a nice favourite with (K♣ 7♠) K♦ alone in the pot against (7♥ 4♦ 2♠). The compensation for the low is that you are stuck there until the end with your high.

Odds against making a Low by	Card 5	Card 5 or 6	Card 5, 6 or 7
Starting with 3 to a low	13/2	3/1	9/5*
Starting with 4 to a low	2/1	4/5	3/7
Holding 3 to a low in 4 cards	-	6/1	3/1*

*These include those hands where you would have hit the low in the last two cards. Of course, in real life, you may have passed earlier.

In limit poker the pots are not stacked in neat piles. The game is played extremely rapidly. It is difficult to know how much money is in the pot. You must keep track of the cards passed and the reactions of your opponents. Meanwhile, the cocktail waitress may want a tip and there may be various other distractions. Limit seems smaller than pot limit or no limit, but you can still lose with appalling rapidity.

Omaha Eight or Better

This is four card Omaha with two blinds. It is played like Straight High, but now the best high and best low split the pot. Of course, a player can use two of his cards to go low and two others to go high.

Example 1

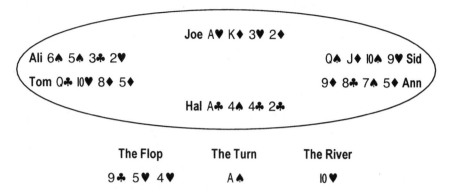

Joe A♥ K♦ 3♥ 2♦

Ali 6♠ 5♠ 3♣ 2♥

Q♠ J♦ 10♠ 9♥ Sid

Tom Q♣ 10♥ 8♦ 5♦

9♦ 8♣ 7♠ 5♦ Ann

Hal A♣ 4♠ 4♣ 2♣

The Flop	The Turn	The River
9♣ 5♥ 4♥	A♠	10♥

Ann puts in the forced small blind of $10 and Hal the big blind of $20. Tom passes. Ali calls $20. Joe calls $20. Sid calls $20. Ann calls for $10. Hal raises $20. Ali, Joe and Sid call. Ann passes. The pot is $180.

The Flop: 9♣ 5♥ 4♥

Hal bets $20. Ali calls. Joe raises $20. Sid passes. Hal and Ali call. The pot is $300.

The Turn: 9♣ 5♥ 4♥ A♠

Hal checks. Ali bets $40. Joe raises $40. Hal passes. Ali raises and Joe re-raises. Ali calls. The pot is $620.

The River: 9♣ 5♥ 4♥ A♠ 10♥

Ali checks. Joe bets $40. Ali calls. The pot is $700. Joe has A♥ 3♥ 5♥ 4♥ 10♥ for high and 3♥ 2♦ 5♥ 4♥ A♠ (the wheel) for low. Ali has 3♣ 2♥ 5♥ 4♥ A♠ (the wheel) for both high and low.

Thus Joe wins half the low and *all* of the high. He gets three-quarters of the pot $525. Ali receives just $175. The expression is, 'he has been quartered off'.

WARNING: In high-low it is not uncommon to receive only quarter of the pot. Try to avoid those situations!

Tom was dealt a turkey and had nothing to think about. Joe has quite a good hand, but felt that there was no need to raise. Sid has quite a good hand, but it is only going high. He needs a very specific flop. Ann thought, 'Well, it's only $10 more.' Hal sensed some players might be coasting in with mediocre hands and raised with his moderate holding, although I might not have done so. He has bad position. The others all called, except Ann who came to her senses and quit the pot. The best cards that can come for her are 6 4 3. Then she would only get half the pot. It would be certain somebody had a low.

TIP: If you raise at Omaha and push a player out, the play is vindicated.

The flop was very active. Hal has trip fours and A 2 towards the best low. He bet and Ali called. Joe has done even better. He has A, 2 or 3 for the best low and also has the nut flush draw and several straights to make. Ali can also make several straights, but needs an ace next card.

An ace duly arrives on the turn. Hal guesses that at least one player has made a straight and also holds an ace. He checks. Ali has made the nut straight, going higher if a 7, 3 or 2 come. He bets. Joe has also made the nut straight and he can improve with a heart. He raises. Fearing a war, Hal gives up on his trips. He may have to pay $160 to see the river card. Ali puts in another raise and Joe yet another one. Ali settles down and calls.

On the river the heart duly arrives. Resignedly, Ali knows that he is almost certainly losing the high, but has to call anyway. He receives back $175, but has put $280 in the pot. He has *lost* $105.

Did Ali ever have a way out? Only by not playing that evening. He could have put in fewer raises and thus lost less. Had a 7, 3 or 2 other than a heart (seven cards) come on the river, then Joe would have been quartered off instead.

TIP: Poker is very volatile. If you can't stand the heat – get out of the game!

Example 2

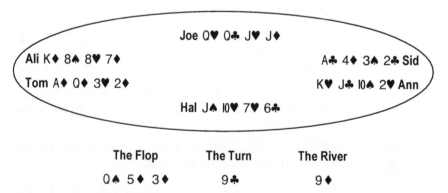

The Flop	The Turn	The River
Q♠ 5♦ 3♦	9♣	9♦

Hal opens the forced bet for $1. Tom makes the forced $2 bet. Ali passes. Joe calls $2. Sid raises $2. Ann and Hal pass. Tom and Joe call. The pot is $13.

The Flop: Q♠ 5♦ 3♦

Tom bets $2. Joe calls. Sid raises $2. Tom raises $2. Joe calls. Sid re-raises $2. Tom and Joe both call. The pot is $37.

The Turn: Q♠ 5♦ 3♦ 9♣

Tom checks. Joe bets $4 and Sid and Tom call. The pot is $49.

The River: Q♠ 5♦ 3♦ 9♣ 9♦

Tom checks. Joe bets $4. Sid passes and Tom calls. The pot is $57. Joe has Q♥ Q♣ Q♠ 9♣ 9♦ for high. Tom has A♦ 2♦ 5♦ 3♦ 9♦ for high. Joe wins the whole $57.

Before the flop Ali's starting hand is worthless. Joe has a good high, but must hit his flop. Sid has a premium hand and raises. Hal would probably call at straight high, but his hand is useless at high-low. Only Tom and Joe have hands worth considering.

On the flop both Sid and Tom have excellent draws. Note that Joe has the nut trips, but he is not yet excited. If a low comes next card, he will only be drawing for half the pot.

There is no change on the turn and now Joe's hand has become much more valuable. There are many cards with which he can lose, but he correctly perceives that Sid and Tom have similar hands. They both call his $4 bet, risking the minimum.

On the river Sid's hand is a total bust. He can pass with a clear conscience. Tom has made the nut flush. He cannot be certain that Joe has a full house. It is reasonable to call $4 in the hope of winning $53.

Odds of making a Low taking the Hand to the River

Holding	The Flop	The Turn	The River
A 4 3 2	13/2	9/5	4/5*
A J 3 2	7/1	2/1	evens*
A Q J 2	12/1	4/1	8/5*

*These include the possibility of making the low with only one low card showing on the flop. Frequently you will pass before getting the chance to make the low.

Odds of making a Low

| Holding | Assume a Flop of Q 8 7 | | Assume a Flop of Q 9 7 |
	The Turn	The Turn and/or the River	On the River
A 4 3 2	5/4	3/7	3/1
A J 3 2	11/10	2/5	3/1
A K J 2	2/1	2/3	5/1

Holdings before the Flop

Only one hand is worth more than one raise before the flop: some-thing such as A♠ A♥ 3♠ 2♥. This game must be played much tighter than Omaha High. 9♥ 8♠ 7♥ 6♠ is unplayable. K♠ Q♥ J♠ 10♥ is fine. Should your ship come in, there will be no low to split the pot with you. A♠ A♥ 10♥ 9♣ is nothing much at all. If your ace comes on the flop, there will probably be a low at the conclusion of the pot. Thus you will receive back at best half of it.

You cannot sit and wait for A 2 forever. Hands such as A♠ Q♦ J♠ 3♥, A♠ Q♦ 4♠ 3♥, Q♥ Q♦ 3♥ 2♦, 6♠ 4♣ 3♠ 2♦, J♠ J♥ 10♦ 8♣ can all take the flop. Two players who put in all the raises probably both have A A 2. Thus they are heavily duplicated.

The Flop

If there are no low cards on the flop, can your hand win in some other way? The flop is 10 9 9. If you have an over-pair or even just a 10, it is quite possible that you are winning.

Position is tremendously important in this game. Perhaps you are last to speak in a four-handed pot. Everybody checks to you. A bet may se-cure the prize, even though you have absolutely nothing.

TIP: Position is enormously important in Omaha Eight or Better.

Example 1: The flop is Q J 7

You hold A 4 3 2. You are 3/1 against making the low by the river. But you have nothing for the high and may split the low. The odds need to be superior to 6/1 to call just to take a shot at the low.

A Q 9 2 is a much better hand. You may be winning and still have a shot at a low, even though it is 5/1 against.

A Q 6 3 is better still. You are now only 3/1 against that elusive low. This may even be worth a raise in order to discourage a potential op-ponent who holds A 2.

A K 10 2 is a super hand. 13 cards to make straights and 20 cards to back into a nut low draw.

This is limit poker and slow-playing your hands is ill-advised. Q Q 5 2 wants to put the maximum in here and now.

Example 2: The flop is Q 7 2

You hold A K J 3. Now you are odds on to make the low by the river. Beware if the turn shows Q 7 2 3. You have been duplicated and hold only a pair of treys.

The turn brings Q 7 2 8. Before it gets to you there is a bet and raise. Oh dear! You have made the nut low, but you are probably only going to get a quarter of the pot. If the pot is small enough, it may be correct to pass. It is unwise to raise. The player who has you beaten for high is just going to win more money.

TIP: Always be on the lookout for a hand that may go both ways. Potential straights and flushes are the things that are going to put the money in the bank.

Example 3: The flop is 8♠ 7♣ 3♠

You hold A♥ K♠ 7♥ 4♠. Before it gets to you there is a bet. Should you pass, call or raise? This is a poker game. It is your task to decide how good your opponent's hand is. If there was a raise before the flop, then somebody probably has your low beaten. You have a pretty good flush draw, but not the nuts. You have a pair and can make two pair, which may be fairly solid. A call seems the most likely play (but other players would say you should pass).

You hold A♠ 6♠ 5♣ 2♣. This is so good, you might just call if somebody has already bet. You want more callers in the pot, in case a magic spade, four or nine hits the table. If an ace or deuce comes, it can all turn to ashes. You would no longer have the nut low.

You hold 10♠ 9♠ 8♥ 8♣. Again you want plenty of callers, yet your hand is still vulnerable. You can only win half the pot. The pot should have been tiny before the flop, otherwise you would have passed.

Example 4: The turn is K♥ 7♠ 2♥ 3♠

You hold A♥ 6♠ 4♠ 4♦. There is a good chance that you are the lone holder of the best low. In addition, you have a backdoor spade flush draw and a five will give you the nut straight. Provided there are more than two players in the pot, it is okay to put in all the raises. With only two players, remember that you only hold a pair of fours for high. There is no sense in going to war. In limit poker, holding the lone ace of hearts means very little. Bluffing the nut heart flush is not going to work.

You hold A♥ K♦ 3♥ 2♣. You have probably been quite active on the flop. Now you have been duplicated and have no low. You will have to grit your teeth and hope to make the nut flush or a full house. Don't despair. You may well be winning the high.

You hold K♦ 8♣ 5♦ 4♣. Presumably you were the big blind and there was no raise. Otherwise, how did you be involved? It was not unreasonable to take a stab at this pot on the flop for just a bet. It would be no great surprise if you were winning both ways – if nobody seems interested. If two people start betting and raising, it is best to pass.

You hold K♦ K♣ l0♥ 9♠. Opinions would differ on whether you should have put in a number of raises on the flop. The trouble is, there are so many ways your high can be outdrawn. In limit there was never any way in which you could protect your hand on the flop. The other side of the coin is that there is no way anyone can now drive you out.

The river tends to play itself automatically in this game. Your odds are likely to be too large ever to consider passing. Just try to avoid being quartered off and raising just with the nut low.

Pot Limit

These, and other high-low games, are played pot limit. The following is the most special consideration:

Let us assume that the pot is $1000 and all the cards are out. Your opponent bets $1000. You think it likely that you are only going to secure quarter of the pot. Then, if you call, you will receive back only $750. It is a *losing* proposition to call just to get a quarter of the pot.

Tip: In pot limit, pass if you expect to be quartered off.

Example

The board is A♦ A♥ 4♦ Q♥ 7♥.

You hold 7♣ 5♣ 3♦ 2♦. Matters can even get worse. A player has bet at the river and somebody has called before you. It is entirely possible that you may end up with just one sixth of the pot. Then you must pass. Sometimes it is correct to pass second in hand in this position. You cannot rely on the next player reading the situation correctly.

You hold A♣ Q♠ 9♠ 2♣. Two-handed you should bet the whole pot. It is extremely unlikely that your opponent has the nut full house with you. He may pass 3 2 for fear of being quartered off. Three-handed or with even more players it may be better to bet perhaps half the pot. Then two or more opponents may call and you can divide up their money. Become very scared if somebody back-raises you. He may have A Q 6 3. If you run into such a brick wall, be philosophical. It happens at poker.

I have concentrated on this aspect in Omaha. However it can also happen in Stud or other variations. It is just so much more common in Omaha, and even more so in Five Card Omaha.

Example: Seven Stud

You hold (8♠ 4♥) 7♥ 3♠ 2♦ against (? ?) K♣ 9♠ 9♥. Your opponent bet third street and he under-bet the pot fourth street. Now he checks to you. Bet the pot. You are putting him under intolerable pressure. If the pot is $10, you can bet $10, then $30 and finally $90. It is going to cost him $100 for $5 profit. If you hold (8♠ 2♥) 7♥ 3♠ 2♦, a pot bet should similarly bluff him out effortlessly.

Say you hold (K♦ 9♣) K♣ 9♠ 9♥ against that tremendous-looking low. Then the correct move is to check-raise $30. He may have paired up and you must make him pay to try to improve to win half the pot.

TIP: You may make the hand one way and not be under threat. Then you can put your opponent(s) under tremendous pressure with cards to come.

Many of these considerations have already been discussed in the limit form of the game. Some players are surprisingly willing to heave large sums into the pot. Yet I may already have advised you to pass such a hand at limit.

Try It Yourself

In each case what should you do at limit and pot limit?

1) Seven Stud Eight or Better. The low card has bet, king has raised, seven called, two re-raised. An ace has yet to act.

a) (8♦ 3♣) 6♦; b) (5♣ 4♣) 3♣; c) (6♥ 6♦) 6♠; d) (9♠ 9♦) A♣; e) (9♥ 8♥) 7♦.

2) Seven Stud Eight or Better. You hold (8♠ 6♠) 7♠ 5♠. Your only opponent with (? ?) K♦ J♣ bets.

3) Omaha Eight or Better. Before it gets to you, the hand has been raised, called and re-raised.

a) A♦ A♣ 3♣ 2♦; b) A♦ 6♥ 5♦ 4♣; c) K♣ Q♦ J♣ 10♦; d) A♦ A♣ 9♣ 8♠; e) A♣ 4♦ 3♣ 2♠.

4) Omaha Eight or Better. The flop is Q♥ 7♠ 4♦. You are first to speak.

a) Q♦ Q♣ A♦ 2♣; b) A♦ Q♣ 5♣ 2♦; c) A♦ K♣ 6♦ 5♣; d) A♦ K♣ 3♦ 2♠; e) 4♥ 4♦ 3♣ 2♦.

5) Omaha Eight or Better. The board is Q♥ 7♠ 4♦ 9♥ 3♦. Your opponent has bet throughout. He now bets out.

a) A♥ 5♥ 3♣ 2♦; b) A♥ Q♠ 4♦ 2♥.

Answers on Page 157.

Chapter Eight

Bluffing

- ♣ **Basic Principles of Bluffing**

- ♣ **How often should you Bluff?**

- ♣ **Try it Yourself**

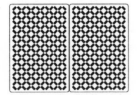 

Outsiders are often under the impression that poker is all about bluffing. Indeed it is the essence of the game. However, when you first play, very few bluffs will stand up. Generally people want to sleep peacefully at night, and they are more likely to do so if they are not worried that they were bluffed out.

NOTE: It is easier to bluff out a strong player than a weak one.

Naturally in limit poker, it is very difficult to bluff at the end of the pot. The odds are just too good. A $4 bet into a $100 pot is sending a boy on a man's errand.

Some players think you should bluff in order to advertise. If you are caught, then you are telling the world you are a loose player. Now, when you are strong, you will be called. There is some truth in this. However, there is a greater truth. It will be years before you play opponents who are good enough to notice!

TIP: Every bet should be made with the idea of winning the pot.

Basic Principles of Bluffing

- Position is very valuable. When players check they are more likely to be weak than strong.

- The more players in the pot, the tougher it is to run a bluff.

- It is very difficult to bluff if your opponent has good odds.

- You may be able to set the scene for a bluff. In Seven Stud you hold (7♠ 6♦) 7♥ 2♥. A bet here will look like a flush if you hit a heart. You need to make sure you both have enough money to bet all the way.

- You hold key cards: in Omaha, the bare A♥ with a flop of K♥ 7♥ 2♥; in Hold 'Em J J and a board of K Q 10 7 3; in London Low-Ball you start with (6 6) 6.

- When bluffing it is good to have outs. That is, there are still cards to come which will leave you a winner. In Omaha you hold A♥ J♠ J♣ 6♥. The flop is K♣ Q♥ 9♠. If you bluff, a 10 may come anyway if called.

- A check-raise usually represents a very strong hand. It is an expensive bluffing strategy and causes your opponent to slow down and think.

- Opponents who are level are easier to bluff than winners or losers. In addition, players who are level are themselves less likely to bluff.

- Sometimes you are quite weak, but think your opponent is bluffing. Then it is often better to raise rather than just call.

- Players are less likely to bluff if they have a little something to show down. Thus, in Deuce to Seven, both players in the pot buy one card. Each is less likely to bluff with K 7 6 3 2 than 7 6 6 3 2. With the former hand, 16 cards give the opponent an even worse hand.

- Players prefer to play rather than to pass. A bluff will always be called more often than game theory dictates.

How often should you Bluff?

Reuben's Theorem

(Read no further unless you are mathematically inclined.)

Bluff percentage = <u>Probability of actually making your hand</u>
odds your opponent is receiving to call

Thus in draw you call to take one card to make a flush. You are 4/1 against making the flush. The probability is 20%. It is pot limit, so you intend to bet the pot. Your opponent is getting 2/1 for his money if he calls your bet. Bluff percentage is 20/2 = 10%.

In Seven Stud you hold (A♦ A♣) 9♣ 7♥ 4♠ A♠ against (? ?) 8♦ K♦ Q♦ 2♦.

It is approximately 3/1 against making the full house or quad aces. This is 25%. At pot limit the bluff percentage is 25/2 = 12.5%. Be warned. This strategy can only work against good players. Weaker ones will always call, smiling weakly, 'I had to call with a flush.' This is better for you. There is no need ever to bluff.

At Deuce to Seven Lowball you hold K 7 4 3 2 against an opponent who stood pat. The pot is $100. You intend to bet $500 if you buy an eight, six or five after throwing the king. How often should you bluff?

You have 12 cards to make the hand you are aiming for. Percentage = 25%. The odds your opponent receives are $600/500 = 1.2. The bluff percentage is 25/1.2 = 20% approximately.

Dave Sklansky has said, 'One of the main defects players have in no limit is that they do not bluff *often* enough.'

What do I mean by perfect strategy? This occurs when an opponent who calls exactly the correct percentage of the time. However, we know that most of our opponents will call more frequently than they should. You will then bluff less often. Some people can always be knocked over. They must be bluffed all the time.

How on earth could you know when to bluff using this equation? Well, take our Deuce to Seven Lowball example. You held K 7 4 3 2. Why not bluff every time you hit a 7, 4 or 3? That is nearly right.

Demonstration of Reuben's Theorem

In our Stud hand we improve 25% of the time. The odds against making our hand are 3/1. The pot is $100 and our opponent bets $100. Thus we are receiving only 2/1 odds. 25% of the time we will bet $300 when we make our hand. 12.5% we will bluff $300. How does this work out in 100 hands?

Profit Calculation

a) Opponent always passes. Win 37.5 x 200. Lose 67.5x 100.

Profit $750

b) Opponent always calls. Win 25 x 500. Lose 12.5 x 400 + 67.5 x 100.
Profit $750

No matter what our perfect opponent does, we will make $7.50 per hand. He will win $92.50 per hand. Our joint profits come from the original $100 in the pot. How can you do that randomly? Why not look at the second hand on your watch? If it is in the first six seconds of the minute, then bluff. Please though, remember sometimes to look at your watch when you have no intention of bluffing!

Let us take one last look at trying to bluff in a limit game. There is $90 in the pot and we can bet $10. Our opponent will get 10/1 odds.

We are trying to make a hand which comes up 20% of the time. The bluff percentage is 20/10 = 2%.

One hand in 50! You need an opponent who is so strong, he will probably recognise you are trying it on anyway. That is not the whole story. If you start your bluff on card five of a Seven Card Stud hand, then he is going to have to put in $30 to see it through. Thus he is betting $30 to win $120. That still permits a bluff only 5% of the time.

Try It Yourself

1. Playing in an average home game, how often should you bluff? a) 30%; b) 10%; or c) never.

2. Playing pot limit against a class player, what percentage of the time should you bluff if you are due to make your hand 30% of the time? a) 30%; b) 15%; c) never.

3. In order, which type of player are you most likely to be able to bluff? a) one who is winning; b) one who is level; c) one who is losing.

4. You are 4/1 against making your hand. Your competent opponent bets the pot. Should you a) pass; b) call; or c) raise?

5. In no limit you have a hand you think is winning but it is not that strong. The pot is $100 and you have $500 left. What should you bet? a) $50; b) $100; c) $200; d) more than $200.

Answers on Page 159.

Chapter Nine

The Opposition

- ♣ Types of Player

- ♣ Reading the Opposition

- ♣ Playing Poker without Cards

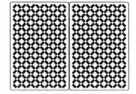 

Types of Player

Basically poker players can be divided into four groups. In ascending order of strength they are:

Soft, loose players are the easiest to beat. They are the meek who certainly do not inherit the earth. We can bet freely at them and they will call with any old rubbish. They will seldom fight back by betting or raising. It is as if they were playing poker with both hands tied behind their back. Of course, we must not be stupid and try to bluff them out.

Soft, tight players are better. When you bet and they call, watch out. They may well have you beaten. With cards to come, you are still being given the opportunity to outdraw them. You will have to assess whether you can bluff them out or will have to show down your hand. Thus they are playing poker with just one hand tied behind their back.

Hard, loose players are much more dangerous. You will lose more money to them than any other type. The trick is also to win more. They will not hesitate to raise if they believe they can take the pot away from you. It is as if they are playing poker swinging all the time with both fists. Sometimes you counter-bluff, only to find they have a good hand.

Hard, tight players are the most dangerous species. They will choose their moments with care and they may be bluffing or holding a monster. They will not be waltzing around in the pot, calling with a mediocre holding. It is as if they are boxing champions, prepared to defend or attack, as necessary. Often such players, when together in a game, tacitly collude. They seek confrontation with other players, not each other.

It is also worth noting two other categories:

Boss players are another, small group. They want to have everybody in the game pay attention primarily to them. They have to play loose, or people won't be focusing on them. When I used mainly to play Seven Stud pot limit, I grew to cultivate such an image. I believed people would otherwise not want to carry on playing against me. They had to be persuaded to see me as the man to beat. Such image-making is often solely an ego trip. It may have nothing to do with maximising profits. Our boxing analogy is one of a player who wants to appear to be flailing wildly. In reality he is actually keeping up a good defence when the going gets rough.

Anonymous players form a sixth group. They want never to be noticed. They have to play tight or too many people will focus on them. Our boxing analogy breaks down with such players. It is impossible to write about the game and maintain such an image.

Of course, few players fit perfectly into the first four neat, specific categories. During an evening, a player may switch moods several times. If you can do this deliberately it can be a winning strategy. The problems arise when your mood is dominated by how you are faring at the table.

Image

You will find that you frequently play with the same group of people. I have been playing against some opponents for nearly 40 years and have been playing in the same game at the Grosvenor Victoria Club since 1989. Three of the current players remain from the beginning, while other regulars have been playing for many years. No one hand is going to change our image of each other now. I have found my own original techniques being played right back at me at a later date. However, it will be some time before *you* even have a style of play.

I find it very pleasant to play in a new game where I do not know the players. In the same position some people complain, 'but I don't know where they are at.' Perhaps they are overlooking the fact that the opposition does not know them either.

It would be nice to be able to project the image of being soft, loose. The problem is, the only easy way to do that is to play precisely that way – and it is costly.

Sometimes there is no problem in projecting the image of being soft, tight. The cards will do that for you. If you can manage this image, then your bluffs will be highly successful. They will be infrequent, but then you will not play in many pots.

Especially when you are new to a game, it can be easy to appear loose and yet in reality be strong. Just push out the boat on your good hands when you have a good run of cards.

The great problem is that the image you do not want to project, that of hard, tight, is also the most reliable winner.

A great deal of talking goes on in poker games. I first played $30-60 limit Seven Stud in Las Vegas in 1974. I confided loudly to a player that one should always start with at least a pair of queens. After all, jacks up is only an average two pair. In those days foreigners were a great rarity in big games. Everybody listened. It took some time before they noticed that this was not my style at all – and talk is cheap. Note the element of truth, that makes nonsense more believable.

Sometimes players show their hole cards when they have no need to do so. Everybody passes and they triumphantly display a bluff. Alternatively, they may put the opposition out of their misery and show their strong hand. Some players show some of their cards – as a tease I suppose.

Unsurprisingly, I never have as many good hands as I would like. Thus I seldom show my bluffs. I prefer my opponents to think that I always have a good hand. Anyway, it can be bad manners. I seldom show my good hands either. Why should I help my opponents feel that they have played well? However, if you do show, then it must be sounder to display your good hands. Then your bluffs have a better chance of standing up.

Sometimes in a pot you feign weakness. This may be partially true. You act slowly because you do not know what to do and check or bet substantially less than the pot. This creates a problem. When your opponent acts strongly you do not know what to think. Is it because of your perceived weakness or because he has a strong hand?

Certain types of players have a stereotyped image of which they can take advantage. Anytime an opponent thinks illogically it must be to your advantage.

Women are usually assumed to be soft. Men think they can bluff them out, while assuming that females don't understand the odds and will play too loosely. They will only bet when they have their hand. Certain men are macho and believe they should never lose a pot to a woman. Such stereotyping can be expensive.

Young players are assumed to be naïve. I advised a friend of mine to shave off his beard in order to look younger. In fact, although lacking in experience, young players often play with great technical subtlety.

Strangers to a game are assumed to be mugs, especially if they have strong accents. If you are new to a game, it is good to feign ignorance of some of the rules. Naturally it is also essential actually to know those rules. Do not go out of your way to seem absurdly ignorant. People resent being taken for a ride. The regulars and staff should try to make you feel at home. Well, so indeed you will, if you win their money.

Moneybags Sitting in a small game with a huge sum of money and acting the boss has peculiar effects. It may cause players to fire after you. They assume that you are just trying to run over the game. Doing this, I have so intimidated players that they have quit until I left. That is a disastrous scenario.

Mike Caro has told the story of how he played in a limit Draw game. He raised before the draw and stood pat. Then, after everybody checked to him, he also checked and showed rubbish. For the cost of two small bets, news of this insanity was spread far and wide.

The late Ted Isles and an associate used to run a game where they cut the pot 5%. One evening Ted was surprised to see his associate, a tight player, voluntarily bet 5/- (five old shillings) blind. Going through the accounts of the night, Ted noticed an item, 'advertising' 5/-.

I play sufficiently foolishly sufficiently frequently that I do not need a separate advertising budget. All I have to do is declare my hand at the conclusion of the pot. Some people are too embarrassed by their errors. If you want to advertise far and wide what an idiot I am, be my guest. After writing these lines I had two encounters with Phil Hellmuth on the Isle of Man. In the first I won all-in with only five outs. In the second he flopped trip aces against my pair. Nothing daunted, it was he who eventually had to outdraw me to split the pot with a board of A K Q J 10. He expressed some distaste for the outcome. I pointed out that he would have to be stupid to come all the way to Britain to play with good players.

A Little Story

Recently I played the following Omaha hand. Initially my motives were obscure to me. I have since realised that they were partly due to my wishing to convey an unusual image.

There was $200 in the pot before the flop.

The flop was Q♥ 7♦ 3♦. I held J♠ J♦ 9♦ 2♥.

The first two players in the pot checked. Only 'The Fisherman' was to follow. I bet $200. The Fisherman called and the other two players passed.

The turn brought Q♥ 7♦ 3♦ 4♣.

I checked. The Fisherman bet $600 and I called.

The river came up Q♥ 7♦ 3♦ 4♣ K♠.

I checked. The Fisherman bet $1800 all-in and I called. He said, 'you win.' I showed down my pair of jacks and did not want to see his cards. After all, he might have made a mistake!

My initial bet was a semi-bluff in the steal position. I might have been winning and, if not, I might make a winning flush. It is often better to bluff late in hand rather than actually on the button. That can be too obvious a bluff.

There was a possible straight on the turn. Naturally I checked. When he bet, I clearly called because I thought I was winning. It is impossible for me to draw the nuts.

Nothing much changed on the river. If he had nothing, but had now made a pair of kings, that would have been unlucky. I again called.

It cost me $2400 to run down the bluff in order to win $3000. That is little better than even money.

Naturally, this set people talking and thinking at the table. I heard one player comment quietly to another, 'Well, he clearly didn't think he had a straight. I don't think it was a good call. He might have lost to a pair of kings.' This was clearly not an analysis for my benefit.

Was my call then a fit of bravado wanting to be a hero? I think not. I am going to pass such hands nearly all the time, perhaps 95%. If my opponents realise this, they are more likely to try to bluff me. Here I was conveying a very clear image with a clear message, 'Bluff me at your peril.' It is so much easier to win at poker if your opponents can be cowed into being soft, weak.

Reading the Opponent

Much of the following relates to pot limit or no limit. Nonetheless, squeezing out an extra bet or saving one at limit is enormously important. Indeed such actions can be easier in that form of the game.

We have all heard the term 'poker face'. Nobody acts like a perfect robot, no matter how experienced they are. The basic premise of Mike Caro's *Book of Tells* is that when somebody shows strength, they are weak. When somebody gives out a signal of weakness, they are strong.

 ### TIP: Mike Caro's Theorem: Weak means Strong; Strong means Weak

Maybe that used to be true in the States where play-acting has always been legal. In England 'moody' used not to be permitted – and sometimes it still isn't. Then again players usually show their true emotions. Anyway, many people have studied Mike's excellent thoughts on the game and now use reverse psychology.

Betting Tempo

These are among the best indicators:

A player check-raises you. He is unlikely to be bluffing. It is an expensive process and he could not rely on you betting to start with.

A player has been betting aggressively while high in Stud. He hits an improving card and checks. Logic tells us he wants us to improve to call on the river.

A player bets small into a big pot. Either he is very strong and begging for a call, or he is bluffing. It can also be a probing bet. He is willing to pass a big raise.

A player bets into you when you are on a draw, for example one card in Draw poker. Do not raise this player. Either he is bluffing or very strong.

Some players always think for the same length of time before they act. Their speed of reaction cannot then be used as a 'tell'.

Try not to think a long time before calling when there is still betting to come. It means other players can concentrate on observing your mannerisms. Some may gain an advantage in this way, even though not even in the pot. Somebody who dwells for a long time usually has a moderate hand. If he calls, he probably intends to go all the way to the river. It is, of course, okay to think when deciding whether to raise all-in or pass.

One common practice at limit in multi-action pots is to raise with a moderate hand. The objective is to lean on the other moderate hands. You must learn to distinguish this from a genuine top dollar raise.

Somebody who is level is much *less* likely to become involved with a tenuous hand. If a player calls you who is winning, he may be pushing his luck. If he calls when losing, then he may be trying to get level. Anyone in a balanced position is much more likely to pass a hand which could go either way.

Physical Signs

A player may seem to be uninterested in the pot. This usually means either he really has given up or he is very interested indeed. This thus deserves a check with a moderate hand.

Trembling hands are seldom an act. It usually shows a release of tension. The player has drawn a good set of cards.

Biological signs are usually true tells. They are difficult to fake.

A player who reaches for his money as you are preparing to bet probably wants a check. This is a more reliable tell at limit. Confusingly, some players are in a tremendous hurry to play the pot. Then they may call before you have had time to bet.

Announcing a bet with a sad voice probably mean the player is strong.

Don't bet a moderate hand at somebody who grimaces at his last card. Either he is weak and won't call, or is strong and you are losing.

If somebody is breathing faster they may well have a strong hand. Bluffers often try to behave extremely passively.

A player who makes a mistake in the hand, such as betting or checking out of turn, is often strong.

These points may seem irrelevant to limit poker, but that is not so at all. Saving one big bet is a triumph. Avoiding betting into somebody who is either going to pass or raise, is a valuable tool.

If observing body language ever becomes a perfect science, it will destroy poker. Usually you should just follow your gut feeling. You may well make the correct decision and never know why. Just remember that most players are more predisposed to call than pass – and that includes you and I.

Playing Poker without Cards

I was asked to write a section on this intriguing aspect of the game by my schoolboy correspondent. Quite apart from the matters of bluff and counter-bluff, there is money management.

Let us assume that you have a percentage advantage in every monetary transaction. If you risk everything every time, then eventually you will go broke. Certainly you may have become extremely rich in the meantime. However, sooner or later, something will go wrong. Then you will do your pieces. Businessmen who are prepared to take big risks may make a great deal of money. Many lose it all several times. They seem to be prepared to accept such slings and arrows of outrageous fortune. I prefer to operate a ratchet system whereby, having made a profit, I cannot lose it all back. When playing poker seriously, it is essential to decide your own risk profile.

TIP: Avoid being a small favourite or big underdog.

This is a principle often found in Hold 'Em. Consider selling short on the stock market. A share price is $1. It can only sink to nothing. It may rise indefinitely. You may make a small profit or a huge loss.

Bargaining

Bargaining is one of the most common poker skills. The shopkeeper offers to sell you goods at one price. You offer a much lower sum. Perhaps you start walking out of the shop to show your lack of interest. The shopkeeper comes part of the way. Eventually you reach a compromise.

This reached its apogee in 2000 with bids for mobile phone frequencies in Britain. There was a system of closed auctions. Companies made bids which were then revealed. They then made fresh bids for sections of the total wavelength available. This bidding process continued for several months, the costs ever-escalating. If one offered too much, then it would win the bid. This might mean that the whole marketing exercise was unprofitable. If one offered too little, it would have been seen as pointless. Companies dropped out during the process. Games theory experts were called in to help decide the bidding strategy, but the companies should have consulted poker players.

Moodying

Moodying by showing decisiveness can be important. A friend of mine told me of how he was at a business meeting one day and he and his directors were asked, 'What if we offered to buy your company?' Without pausing to think, he said, 'No way. It is not for sale.' His immediate hope was to increase the size of any possible bid. Sadly the company later had to be liquidated. Well, we do not win all our poker hands!

I was involved with the World Chess Championship which was due to take place in London in 1986. The money was coming from the Greater London Council, but I was told one day that its receipt had been blocked by a court order. Later that evening I had dinner with the then President of the World Chess Federation. I told him nothing of our financial problems. We discussed only administrative and technical details of the event. David Anderton was also at the meeting and afterwards he said to me, 'Now I know why you are a good poker player!'

The Allies intended to invade Europe by landing on the Normandy beaches. By feinting, they succeeded in convincing the Germans their intentions lay elsewhere.

The Cold War arms race was arguably the longest and most expensive poker game ever played. The United States and Soviet Union each felt that they had to have at least nuclear equality. If one side developed new weapons, the other had to follow suit. Would they have ever been used? There seems to be no conceivable purpose in unleashing a nuclear holocaust. If my finger was on the red button, knowing Britain was about to be destroyed, retaliation would seem to be utterly futile. I hope I would not be so stupid as to want revenge. A friend of mine once said, 'Oh, but we would have to fight back to show that we could not be pushed around.' He seemed to miss the point that it would be too late to teach anybody a lesson.

The cost of the arms race to both sides was enormous. Perhaps the US won the race. It helped destroy the USSR economy and, with it, their whole way of life. However, the western world was dicing with death. Unleashing nuclear war is not the same as the dealer announcing who has won a poker pot. Anyway, now we are spending money trying to help the Russians rebuild their economy, so that they can then buy more things from us.

The Americans were frightened that Vietnam would become Communist. They fought a long, bitter, expensive and futile war to try to prevent this from happening. Would they not have been better off giving money to the Vietnamese people? Then they would have wanted to be capitalists. This is identical to doing business at the end of a poker hand when there are still cards to come. Losing or winning a few thousand dollars is unimportant. Allowing thousands of people to die is playing with chips that you cannot afford ever to lose.

Chapter Ten

The Mathematics of Poker

- ♣ The Definition of Gambling
- ♣ Probability
- ♣ Odds
- ♣ Serial Betting
- ♣ Implied Odds
- ♣ Are You Winning the Hand?
- ♣ Try it Yourself

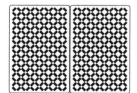

I know many people will shudder the moment odds or probability are mentioned. All the odds you need to know have already been given on the various games. Some of you will want to know more and will not want just to take my word for it.

It is a real shame that gambling theory is not taught in our schools. It is a little like the state of sex education in my youth. By not teaching the subject at school, it was thought we would not indulge. Gambling would be one of the most valuable subjects on the curriculum. It permeates our culture.

The Definition of Gambling

The *Oxford English Dictionary* is not much use. Basically there are two meanings: 'wagering' *or* 'wagering against the odds'.

If the former definition is used, then investing on the stock market is gambling. So, in a sense, is deciding to take three years to do a degree in the hope of eventually earning more money. Yes, I know there are other benefits to be derived from going to university.

If you believe it is wagering against the odds, I just have one piece of advice: *Don't gamble!*

WARNING: Never wager against the odds

If you want to have the occasional flutter, please be my guest or my opponent at the poker table. You are prepared to spend money on going to the theatre or on vacation. Why not spend it on gambling?

If you wager against the odds, eventually you will lose money. Any number of people have told me how they had a whiz of a system against roulette. If you believe them, I will bet you about tossing a coin. Every time it comes down heads you give me a $100. Every time it comes down tails I will give you $99. Go on, try it and send me the money when you have finished.

Odds = (1 – Probability)/Probability

We will return to odds later, after studying probability.

Probability

Probability of making a Hand with One Card to come

This is simply defined as follows: $$\frac{\textbf{number of improving cards}}{\textbf{number of unseen cards}}$$

For example, in Draw you hold Q♥ J♥ 9♥ 2♥ 10♠. You call and take one card. Should you discard the 10♠ to make a flush or the 2♥ to make a straight? You can make a flush with nine cards and the straight with only eight. Moreover, a flush is a superior hand to a straight. There are 47 cards that you have not seen.

The probability of making the flush is 9/47 = 0.19 = 19%.

In Seven Stud you hold (9♠ 9♥) 3♥ 7♥ 9♦ 2♦ against
(? ?) A♣ 6♣ 9♠ J♣. In addition the passed cards are A♦, Q♦, 10♠,
8♥, 6♥, 6♦, 5♣, 4♥ and 4♠.

There are nine cards left with which to make your full house (your
opponent has 9♣). You have seen 19 cards. Thus there are 33 cards
left. We make no distinction between those cards passed unseen and
those still to come.

The probability of making the full house is 9/33 = 27%.

You will note that it is desirable to remember *all* the passed cards.
What seemed irrelevant to start with may become important. In our
example, you need to know the whereabouts of the deuces. If you are
unable to remember all the passed cards, don't worry. Just remember
what you can and treat the others as if they are still in the deck. You
are not giving up that much at Seven Stud High.

Probability of making a Hand with more than One Card to come

This is a much more complex problem. The only correct way is to determine *all* the possible winning and losing hands. An alternative is
to do a computer simulation. Neither of these is practical at the table
or driving home, trying to decide whether you were right to call.

With two cards to come, the probability of making a hand is

**1 – (the probability of not making it next card x the probabil-
ity of not making it last card)**

In Omaha you hold A♥ K♦ 7♦ 2♥. The flop is Q♥ 6♥ 3♣.

You can see seven cards currently. Thus there are 45 left. If you do
not hit a heart next card, then you will have seen one more card.
There will be 44 left. There are nine hearts for you to hit.

The probability of making a heart is:

1 – [(45-9)/45 x (44-9)/44] = 1 – 0.64 = 0.36 = 36%

Note, this is *not* the probability of your *winning* the hand. If an open
pair comes, your opponent may make a full house.

In Seven Stud you hold (J♥ 9♥) 7♥ 3♥. You are up against
(? ?) 8♠ 9♦ and (? ?) A♣ 6♦. In addition the passed cards are
K♦, Q♥, 9♠, 5♣ and 4♠.

You have eight hearts (Q♥ was passed) to hit. This could be any of the
three cards you are to receive. You have seen 13 cards. If you do not
hit a heart next card, then you will have seen 14. Similarly on sixth

street it becomes 15. Thus you will not have seen 39, 38, 37 cards.

The probability of a making a flush is:

$1 - [(39-8)/39 \times (38-8)/38 \times (37-8)/37] = 1 - 0.49 = 51\%$.

You are a small favourite to make your flush. Again, this does not tell us the probability of your winning. One of your opponents may make a better hand. In addition, you may yourself make a full house or even four jacks. Clearly against two opponents you will be happy to put in all of your money at this stage. There is $100 in the pot. With raises, each of the three of you put in $200 all-in on card four. You then only need to win the pot 200/700 of the time to break even. This is 29%.

The probability of winning is:

probability of making hand x probability of opponent(s) not making better hand.

Example

At Seven Stud you hold (K♣ J♣) 9♣ 6♣ 7♦ 4♠ against what you imagine to be (A Q) Q♥ 9♦ 4♥ A♥. Your opponent bets. You have seen K♠, 8♠, 3♥, 3♦, 2♦, 2♣. Why you should guess he has aces up is between you and your brain. Thus you will win with a club, *unless* he hits a full house.

There are eight clubs you have not seen. You have seen 16 cards, which leaves 36.

Probability of making club flush is 8/36.

Probability of his not improving is (36-4)/36.

Probability of winning is $(8 \times 32)/(36 \times 36) = 20\%$.

In the cases where you have the made hand, you work in reverse.

Such calculations are impossible at Omaha before the flop. The odds of 8♥ 7♠ 6♠ 5♥ against what you imagine to be aces cannot be determined arithmetically. Only a computer simulation can help. I do not know of any program where you can choose random aces together with two random cards each hand. Four running cards double-suited against aces win better than 33% of the hands. If up against two players, both with aces, you probably have the best of it.

Obviously, the more players you are up against, the better odds you have. However, there is a greater likelihood of one of them coming over the top and beating you.

Odds

Most books quote the probability of your winning a hand. I have always found it easier to work with the odds. Reiterating:

Odds = **(1 - Probability)/ Probability** *or*

(100 - Probability)/Probability

(when working in percentages)

If the probability of your winning is 0.33, the odds against winning are (1-0.33)/0.33 = 2/1.

If the probability of your winning is 0.6, the odds against winning are (1-0.6)/0.6 = 2/3, that is, you are favourite.

The pot is $250. Your opponent bets $100. You are receiving 3.5/1. You estimate your hand is 3/1 against, 25% probability of winning. You *must* call. Otherwise you are giving too much away.

Serial Betting

Here is one of the biggest mistakes people make. The game is limit Razz and it is $2 to you on fifth street. You guess you are 4/1 against winning the hand by the river and the pot is $11. Should you call?

Your opponent has bet $2 and he will again bet $2 on sixth street. The total you can win is then $13. It is going to cost you $4. Thus you are receiving 13/4 for your money. The correct move is to pass.

One of the most common errors at Omaha is to call on the flop to make a nut flush. It is approximately 2/1 against making it by the river. The pot is $10 and your opponent bets $8. Should you call?

You win $18 for $8. Surely, it is obvious, you are getting better than 2/1? *No.* 80% of the time you will not make the hand on the turn. What if he then bets $20? The pot is now $46. Summarising:

	Return	Loss
1 in 5 hands you get $26 back	26	
4 in 5 hands you lose $8		32
1 in 5 hands you get $66 back	66	
4 in 5 hands you lose $20		80

Your return is $92 for every $112 spent.

WARNING: Do not call a pot bet on the flop at Omaha just to make a nut flush. That is, unless the bet is all-in, or there are at least two opponents.

You will note that I have written of guessing and approximate odds. You do not need to know the precise figures. In fact, it is impossible to do so. Poker is not an exact science.

Implied Odds

Let us say the pot is $100 and the bet is $100 to you. Thus you are getting 2/1. But there are two other players in the pot who may call. If they both do so, then you surely will be receiving 4/1? This is extremely dangerous reasoning. Neither may call. Worse still, one may raise. In addition, you would have two more players to beat.

Its is far more important to calculate the likelihood of being called if you make your hand. In limit you are probably going to get a call. In pot limit, you are probably also going to be called, basically because you are inexperienced and playing against fellow beginners.

Thus the pot is $100 and the bet is $100 to you. If you call and make your hand, then you will bet $300. You estimate your opponent will call. Your win expectancy is $500. You are 4/1 against making the hand Thus you should now call. You have assumed that he is going to call your bet on the end. Bluffing, if you fail to make the hand, would be very confused thinking.

If the game is no limit, then you may think you can always justify a call. This is not so. Once you are playing that game – not yet I hope – players are much more likely to pass.

TIP: Many players do not have the guts to make a very big bluff.

You must also worry about the situations where your opponent re-draws. That is, he makes a hand even better than you have drawn. This can be extremely costly.

TIP: If in doubt at limit call; If in doubt at pot limit usually pass; If in doubt at no limit pass.

Are you winning the Hand?

In pot limit there is often a combustion point with cards to come. Your decision should be either to pass or to raise all-in. The following is the ultimate nightmare scenario. You call, then call on the last card, only to discover that your opponent has outdrawn you. Then you realise to your horror that he would have passed had you raised.

TIP: It is often best to pass or raise. Calling is the worst option.

Try It Yourself

Where a figure is asked for, why not try first making a guess and then working it out? At the table you will seldom be able to afford the luxury of a precise calculation.

1. The flop is 9♥ 5♠ 2♥ with a pot of $100.

At no limit Hold 'Em you hold A♥ J♥ and come out betting $200. Your only opponent raises $1000 and has $1000 left.

a) What are the odds against your winning if he holds 10 9?

b) What are the odds against your winning if he holds A 9?

c) What are the odds against your winning if he holds trips?

d) What action should you take in i) a money game; ii) a tournament?

2. The flop is 9♥ 7♠ 3♥ with a pot of $100.

At pot limit Omaha you hold A♥ 10♣ 6♣ 5♥ and your first opponent comes out betting $100. There are two players left to act after you and bundles of money on the table.

a) What are the odds against your winning if he holds trip nines?

b) What are the odds against your winning if he has J♥ 10♥ 9♣ 7♦?

c) What action should you take in i) a money game; ii) a tournament?

3. In Seven Stud you hold (9♣ 10♠) J♦ Q♦ and your opponent holds (? ?) A♠ 4♥.

Assume the cards passed are average.

a) What are the odds against your winning if he has (A ?) in the hole?

b) What are the odds against your winning if he has (A 4) in the hole?

c) What action should you take in i) a money limit game; ii) a money pot limit game; iii) a limit tournament; iv) a pot limit tournament?

4. In Deuce to Seven you hold Q 7♠ 5♥ 4♣ 3♦ with a pot of $100.

One player bets $400. Another calls. Thus it is $400 to you.

a) What are the odds against your making i) a nine low or better; ii) an eight low or better; iii) a seven low?

b) What action should you take in i) a money game; ii) a tournament?

5. The flop is Q♥ 4♥ 2♠.

At High-Low Omaha you hold A♥ K♠ J♦ 10♥. Before it comes to you, there is a bet, raise and re-raise.

a) What are the odds against your making the nut flush by the river?

b) What are the odds against your winning the whole pot when the cards are shown?

c) What are the odds against your winning the high, assuming one player holds trips?

d) What action should you take in i) a money limit game; ii) a money pot limit game; iii) a limit tournament; iv) a pot limit tournament?

Answers on Page 159.

Chapter Eleven

The Poker World

- ♣ **The Cost of Playing**

- ♣ **Money Management**

- ♣ **Tournament Play**

- ♣ **Where to Play**

- ♣ **Poker Education and Entertainment**

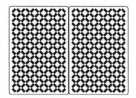 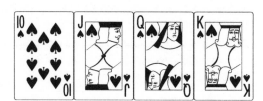

The Cost of Playing

Very few things in life are free. The saying 'There is no such thing as a free lunch,' is incorrect, but close to the truth. This is so for poker as for all other pursuits. You play in a private game in which there are no overheads. Someone must pay for the cleaning, decks of cards, chips, arranging the game and refreshments. Perhaps you each take it in turn, but it mounts up.

When you play in a casino or public card room, there has always to be a charge. How else could the place survive? The money is taken in two ways, either as a percentage of each pot, or a fixed sum per hour. Such a house charge is also known as the cut, rake, table charge or vigorish.

Some places take 5% of each pot and also expect you to tip the dealer 1%. Most hands are two-handed. The pot is $200. You and your opponent have each put in virtually $100 each. Six per cent is raked from the pot, leaving $188. You have won $88 for $100 invested. Thus, every time you win a two-handed pot, the actual charge is about 12%. Such games can be beaten, but it is very hard work. You must play very tight and be a much better player than the opposition. When a high-low pot is split, they usually have the decency to take only 2.5%. You may even almost break even in the hand!

In Las Vegas they take a higher percentage from the smaller games. The rake may be 10%, but this is capped at $3. A typical hand of $5-$10 stud exceeds $100. At 25 hands per hour this will come to $75 plus tips of $25. In the larger games, the charge is usually about $10 per player per hour. It seldom rises above that, no matter how big the game. This is then $80 per table. The dealers must still be tipped at least $1 per hand. Otherwise they will starve. Thus the charge comes to about $12.50 per hour, which is not excessive. It is in the interests of the dealers to deal efficiently and rapidly. If you are a regular professional, you would also be well advised to tip the more senior staff. The cocktail waitresses also have to be tipped, although the beverages are free. Clearly, the bigger the game, the less important the rake.

It is illegal to cut the pot in Britain and also, unfortunately, to toke the staff. Thus the dealers have less incentive to be efficient. The staff have to be paid full salaries. Value Added Tax (17.5%) must be paid on the table charge. The casino must also pay a high license fee and corporation tax on its profits. I am not crying for the casinos, but all this results in higher table charges than in the US. The charges increase with the size of the game. This is bad news for me and other professionals. At the Grosvenor Victoria Casino, the smallest charge is £5 ($7), going up to £25 ($38) each per hour. There is no professional dealer in the former game.

Let us assume that the latter game is played three times a week, 50 weeks of the year, for 10 hours. Eight players each pay £25 per hour. Thus the total table charge per year is £300,000 ($450,000). Of course it is not the same players taking part all the time. In the last two years there has been a float of about 50 different players. However, most are regulars. Where is this money coming from? It is mostly from businessmen or salaried people. They earn money outside the casino and then spend some of it on poker. Some comes from minnows who win in smaller games and then chance their arm in the big game.

Do not take this to mean that the bigger the game, the stronger the players. Some classy players do not like playing in big games, others cannot afford it. Often the *second* biggest game in a card room is the toughest. Certain macho losers can only bring themselves to play in the biggest game in town.

You must be better than even money in a poker game to justify playing for financial gain. This is unsurprising. You need to be a top-class professional at any game to make a good living. Chess, golf and tennis are all individual sports, but none of the top professionals in these sports have to pay entry fees. The prize money is usually provided by sponsors. The overheads in chess are low, but so are the pickings. Golf and tennis provide much richer rewards, but the expenses are also very high.

 NOTE: The total table charges are extremely important in poker.

In the 40 years that I have been playing I estimate I must have paid $500,000 in table money. Many people play much longer sessions than me and more frequently. Had I invested this money wisely, I would be worth much more than I am today. Does this mean paradoxically that I should have invested my table money rather than play? Fortunately, this is not the case. I needed to play in order to earn the amount raked. In addition I have incurred other expenses. Even so, the most important aspect is the fact that I have enjoyed myself.

Money Management

The Significance of Money Management

'Money management is the single most important aspect of winning poker.' Donnacha O'Dea (one of the best Irish players) and also myself.

'Money management is one of those concepts that should have died long ago but didn't and still makes its way into far too much gaming literature.' From *Poker for Dummies* by Richard Harroch and Lou Krieger – at the start of a 15 page chapter on the subject!

How can four authorities have such disparate views? As usual in such cases, we are simply talking at cross-purposes. Of course *fallacious* money management concepts are totally worthless. Indeed they are destructive of your bank balance.

TIP: *The* golden rule of poker: never play with money that you cannot afford to lose.

I have previously emphasised how important it is not to allow outside influences to disturb your play. How can you play objectively if you cannot afford to lose your table stake? You will only be willing to put your money in with a cinch. Most good poker hands are far too marginal for that.

In Anthony Holden's extremely enjoyable book, *Big Deal*, he tells how he flew first class to play in Lafayette, Louisiana. The fare was £2,000 and his total poker bankroll about £8,000. Frankly, that is ridiculous.

TIP: Never allow your expenses to become too high a proportion of what you are playing for.

Sensible Odds

The worst odds you ever receive at poker are slightly better than even money. Frequently the odds actually offered of perhaps 3/1 are inadequate. You call because of the implied odds. That is, the amount you may win if you make your hand. At an early stage of a pot limit or no limit hand, you typically get 2/1 for your money. 8♥ 7♣ cannot face a raise on its own merits. You need the implied odds to justify a call. Received wisdom is that you should not commit more than about 5% of your stack with such a hand. Such opportunities are never forthcoming in a no limit tournament. However, it is okay for you to strike the first raise. This is an ideal bluffing situation. You may win the pot uncontested. If bet at, you would have passed, lacking adequate odds. If raised, you can pass with no qualms. If called, your hand is full of mystery.

In limit poker you may well receive better than 2/1 odds. However, the upside potential is far lower if you hit your hand. It is also extremely easy to be sucked in for the ride because the bets seem so small.

TIP: Your initial calling requirements should be tighter in limit poker than in pot limit or no limit.

Tax

Tax law differs very substantially in Britain and the US. Unfortunately the Americans have not inherited our attitude to gambling. Gambling wins are outside the concept of earned income in Britain. Thus your wins and losses are totally irrelevant to the tax inspectors. Since poker is regarded as gambling, profits are untaxed, a point I had to explain to my tax inspector many years ago. Mansour Matloubi won the big one at the World Series. The British Inland Revenue then tried to tax him. They said poker was his only source of income and that therefore he was professional. The case went to the High Court. Mansour won and the IR did not pursue the matter.

The situation is different in Vegas. The government wants its cut. Should you win much over $1000 on a slot machine, the taxman comes bustling over to take the government's share. If you do not file tax returns in the US, they take 30% on the spot. Isn't it odd that this is never publicised? Your winnings will be reported to the IRS if you do well in a poker tournament. You are allowed to claim your expenses through the year and your losses. However, you will be required to prove the latter. You are not allowed to roll over your losses through more than one tax year. This is quite different from other business expenses. If you are a foreigner and win in a tournament, the organiser is required to take the tax. Some countries like the UK have a reciprocal tax agreement with the US. Then, provided the management has reached an agreement with the IRS, no tax should be taken at source.

When assessing your win-loss probabilities in the US, this tax liability must be factored in. Of course, nobody bothers with small-time players.

This has an unfortunate side-effect in Vegas, since no citizen wants to play solely with chips on the table. They do not want to have to cash them in at the casino cage and therefore play with packs of hundred dollar bills. This slows down the game and also makes it difficult to determine how much money people are playing on.

Poor Money Management

Many of my opponents quit when they are ahead by a small amount but play on when they are losing. Lucky me. This is a recipe for disaster, but *not* because I believe that the cards remember who is winning or losing.

 TIP: Nobody plays as well when losing as when winning.

I have spoken about this phenomenon to professionals in many different sports and they all agree. When they are winning they feel more confident and play better. When losing, they lose confidence and their play deteriorates. In addition, they may steam or go on tilt at poker. That is, over-press their luck in the hope of recouping the losses.

Anyway, this is, to some extent, a self-fulfilling prophecy. Many of your opponents believe in luck. Thus, if you are winning, they expect you to carry on doing so. They lose confidence or their judgement becomes clouded.

A losing player may have a marvellous hand. However, he fails to raise and capitalise on his good fortune. His reason, 'I've been running so bad I didn't want to take the risk.' Naturally the bad run will continue.

When I go to play poker, I nearly always do so for a pre-determined length of time. I am egotistical and believe that I can overcome a bad run. Yet, I am fairly sure that I should quit when losing but carry on playing when winning. Then I would win more.

If you are losing and the game is extremely good, then you should continue playing. That is, provided you feel good. Sometimes I take a big beat in a pot in which I had much the best of it. Sometimes I run into a brick wall. These occurrences seldom faze me. What worries me is when I think I have played a pot badly. I think I am also the only player I know who wins a pot, but is disappointed because I played badly.

WARNING: Never steam and never go on tilt.

Often after losing a big hand a player will push the boat out too far on the next one. Then they lose more and are on a slippery slope to oblivion. People frequently bundle in their last remaining money of the evening in one last desperate fling.

When I have just lost a pot I may be dealt a series of mediocre hands. I then sit back and lick my wounds. My opponents may come to believe I am down and have the wrong perception. If instead I receive a super hand, I play the hell out of it. My opponents may assume that I am on tilt and there we are. Deception in poker is by no means solely about bluffing.

Some players quit if they were winning big and lose half back. This is not so bad. Forget the money, it is self-management.

NOTE: The pain of losing outweighs the pleasure of winning.

I have discussed this with other games players and they agree. You don't want to inflict pain on yourself. Three small losses and one big win may be highly profitable. But who cares, if it makes you unhappy?

Money won or lost at poker is not a soulless statistic in an account ledger. You were winning $1,000 and go home only $100 ahead. Result: sorrow. You were losing $1,000 and go home losing only $100. Result: joy.

Short and Sweet

Many players do not like to play short sessions. They fear starting off a loser and not having time to recover. Since life is just one long poker game, this is nonsense. Very few people realise that optimal play is actually the reverse. If you are losing and have to leave early, then you cannot run your losses. You may end up with a number of small wins. This may be emotionally more satisfying than one big win and several small losses.

Play stops at 4 or 6am in casinos in Britain. On one occasion I doubled my money on the last hand of the evening. There was another table at which there was one last hand to play. As I went to cash in, the floorman commented, 'Why don't you play the last hand there?' I am totally lacking in superstition so I took his advice. I then trebled my money.

TIP: Do not be frightened of short sessions.

Try never to play when ill, tired or upset.

WARNING: Never play when you are off-balance.

Some players deliberately needle their opponents. I think this is disgusting. Why spoil someone else's enjoyment of their game? Moreover, it is ineffective. Players who become upset in such circumstances are probably losers and may well quit the game. It will roll off the backs of winners.

Win Expectancy

I used to keep accurate records of my wins and the number of hours played. Then I had a losing streak and gave it up. That's a pity, because no publicised figures exist on pot limit.

It has often been said that, in a limit game, a good win is one big bet an hour. Thus, you play $10-$20 Hold 'Em or Seven Stud and you could make $20 an hour. This is presumably after table expenses. During play you will have many swings. How big a bankroll do you need to make certain you never go broke?

In his book *Gambling Theory and other Topics*, Mason Malmuth suggests that it should be at least 300 big bets. In our $10-$20 game, that means $6000. It takes that to ensure that you will outlast a bad run. The real truth of the matter is that life is just one big poker game.

NOTE: You will never know how well you did at poker until you quit playing or die.

That is not entirely true. If I ever get even at poker – I will go seriously bankrupt.

I believe that Mason requires too high a safety net. But that is substantially true because of the next piece of advice:

WARNING: Don't give up your day job.

Being solely a professional poker player is very risky, especially if you have expensive luxuries like children. It is extremely desirable to have other sources of income.

What is a good hourly rate in a pot limit game? I really have no idea how you would measure this, since it depends on the volatility of the particular game. I last kept accurate records in the early 1970s when I played Seven Stud. At that time I netted £6 per hour. The minimum buy-in was £50 and I used to sit down with £500. With inflation, to-day's equivalent might be £40 per hour, £350 buy-in and £3500 sit down. It was extremely regular, yet I was also a full-time school-teacher at that time. My hourly rate at that was much lower.

Change Mason's suggestion to 300 times the hourly win rate for limit. My gut feeling is that you need much more to reach his safety level at pot limit. Remember, I believe that his requirements are too high. That does not mean that he is wrong; we simply have different views. Perhaps he would require 1000 x the hourly win rate. The fluctuations in pot limit Omaha are much greater than in pot limit Seven Stud. There are other factors. Unsurprisingly I played better 30 years ago. Seven Stud is more a game of pure skill and in those days my opponents were weaker. There is so much more information available now on how to play poker.

It is for you to decide for yourself what measure of risk you are prepared to take. This is equally true when investing in the stock market. When you are young and poor, you can risk going broke in the hope of winning big. The upside outweighs the downside. If you run out of money, you can always start again. As a wrinkly who is moderately comfortable, that is a no, no for me. Successful poker players tend to like living near the edge. You may prefer to play for such small sums that you can never be hurt. Wins won't figure to matter either. Then, in a sense, poker becomes a purely intellectual exercise. That's okay too.

If you always play for your entire bankroll then, sooner or later, you will go belly-up. This is despite the fact that you have an edge in the game. Inevitably the odds will not always pan out correctly. Thus you should operate a ratchet system and play with only a proportion of your bankroll.

WARNING: Do not play up your entire bankroll.

Have I gone off the rails, writing about playing professionally for people who are starting poker? I think not. When you have a good winning run, you will probably flirt with the idea.

NOTE: Playing expenses ensure that more money is lost at poker than won.

So, on what occasions should you play poker? It's okay if you are an amateur willing to spend some of your hard-earned money or free time on your hobby. Otherwise only play when you expect to win enough to compensate for your time. This depends on the size of the game, the nature of the game and your opponents. If you know the players well, who are the losers? If you cannot see any – it may well be you.

WARNING: You should only play poker when you have an adequate positive expectancy.

Now, come on. I am telling you not to play beyond your means and only to play when you expect to win. How then can anybody ever play in a larger game? You should have funds available from your non-poker work. Also sometimes you should take a flyer. That is, risk what is perhaps a rather high proportion of your capital. If you lose, lick your wounds and regroup. If you win, the oil wells may start gushing.

TIP: It's okay to take a shot at a big game, but be careful.

Maintaining a Sense of Proportion

One major problem for a gambler is that living expenses start to seem unimportant. What does it matter if I buy a new suit? That is just one small pot. Eric Drache was once asked why he always travelled first class by air. 'What difference does it make?' he answered. 'Anyway, who will I find to lend me money in coach?' The wife of one well-known player asked plaintively, 'All the other wives I know work to a budget. Why don't I?'

Of course, the swings in poker are enormous. What you must look at is the overall trend. It does not matter if your results are plus or minus $100 per hour over a short period. What counts is the overall $10 per hour profit.

Some players take this view too far. They become very mean and spend nothing. They are unwilling to fritter their money away on luxuries like food, women and houses. This is just as big a trap. The first function of money is to use it to buy things.

Rushes

This is defined as having a run of good wins well beyond normal statistical expectancy. Nothing would be odder than that each of the eight players around a table wins a hand each consecutively all evening. Thus we do not expect the cards to average out in the short term.

I used to believe absolutely that there was no such thing as a rush. Why should the cards remember what has happened before? My rational viewpoint has never been shaken by the opinions of other players. However, my observations have led me to consider the possibility that I could be wrong. I have seen several players go for years hitting unnatural good fortune. This has even happened to me over shorter periods. I, at least, have been aware that the statistical probabilities were being flouted.

Nothing can beat the strategy of playing badly and luckily. This is an utterly deadly combination. It beats playing well and luckily hands down! Poker is the only game I know where bad play may be rewarded in the short term.

If you could know when your rush was going to start and finish, you would win a fortune. I have heard of players who start pushing the boat out every time they win a pot. They figure it may be the start of a rush and they want to maximise the benefits. Then, as soon as they lose, they hold back. If there were such a thing as a definable rush, this would be a good system.

I have known several players who have come unstuck over the years. They believed that their good wins were due solely to skill, not unnatural luck. They parlayed their wins from a small game to a big one. When the rush stopped, they lost heavily.

Here is one sad but sobering statistic: A majority of the players who have won the World Series final have later gone bankrupt.

A reverse rush is more likely. The table charges are a drain. Occasionally you may be cheated. Thus your natural result, if you are an average player, is a decline in your fortunes.

If your opponents believe that you are on a rush, then it becomes, to some extent, true. They will lose confidence and play in an inferior manner. If you feel down, then a reverse rush will become a reality. Try to represent the mood of a reverse rush. You should be on a winner, if in truth, you are brimming with confidence.

There you are then, if you want to believe in rushes or the tooth fairy, be my guest.

Tournament Play

The Growth of Tournament Poker

Tournaments are a relatively recent innovation, having only started around 1970. There are many differences between tournament and money poker and in this chapter we shall explore these.

In Britain *all* the entry fees are returned as prizes. For example, it costs £100 to enter and there are 100 entries. The total prize fund is then £10,000. In fact, it is not uncommon for the casinos to *add* to the prize fund. Of course, casinos are not charities. It costs a substantial sum to put on an event. There is administration, publicity, loss of revenue from the space taken up and staffing. The tournaments are loss leaders. They attract customers to the venue. The management hopes that punters will lose money at casino games. They should at least pay table charges for future money poker games. In addition, sponsorship is a good form of publicity. Clearly the Grosvenor Victoria Casino in London believes in this marketing plan. They stopped their tournaments, but then reintroduced their weekly small ones and in October 2000 and March 2001 held a big one-week series – the first for some years.

The entry fee for some tournaments, especially outside London, can be very small: £25, £15 or even £10.

Recently Channel 4 in Britain has started a series of Late Night Poker Tournaments. Three had taken place by the end of 2000 and they have been very successful. Poker was very much a minority sport in Britain but it is now rapidly gaining in popularity.

In the US there is a small entry charge, but this used to be waived for the big event at the World Series of Poker. This charge is usually much smaller than the table charge for a money game.

Poker tournaments are also popular in Australia, Austria, the Czech Republic, Finland, France, Germany, Holland, Ireland, Russia and Slovenia. Poker tournaments are also held on cruises, particularly in the Caribbean and off the West Coast. The house percentage tends to be higher in the European countries.

Tournaments are a substantial reason for the growth in popularity of poker. Players feel more secure knowing their total liability. This is simply the amount of the buy-in.

Structure

Basically all tournaments are the same. Everybody buys in for the same amount of chips. Let us take the big one, $10,000 and 500 players. That means the prize fund is $5 million. The entrants play until there is only one player left with all $5 million chips. In the 2000 World Series the winner then received $1,500,000. The player who came second received a pre-announced percentage and so on down. Even the player knocked out 36th won more than $10,000. Prior to 2000 the first prize was 'only' $1 million.

Relatively few of the players pay the $10,000 up front. They enter via satellites in which 10 players put up $1000 and the winner secures his berth. Or 100 players put up $100 – and so on.

In November 2000 Ladbrokes Casino on the Isle of Man ran a major new tournament. with a guaranteed first prize of £1 million. This event was filmed by Sky Television, for world-wide release. In the end there were 157 entrants, each putting up £6000. The total prize money offered was £1,250,000, so in total £4 was given away for every £3 invested. In addition, if you paid up front you were 'comped' for your air fare, hotel bill and food.

Most of these big events are played no limit Hold 'Em, a tradition that is unlikely to change. In other contexts, no limit is not particularly popular.

Both the Ladbrokes and World Series events are longer in duration than any of the others on the calendar. They continue for four days before there is a winner. At the World Series event, typically half are knocked out on the first day, and they then go down to 27 on the second and six on the third. In 2001 the World Series lasted five days.

These poker tournaments with their massive prizes are unique in sport. You need considerable expertise to do well. However, unlike other sports you do not have to prepare for months in advance. Also you are able to continue with your ordinary life immediately. Some players are to be found back in action with their million the following day.

There is another somewhat different way in which some tournaments are played. You might lose all your chips in the first hour but in that case you are allowed to buy in again for the same amount. Thus there might be 50 entries, each of $100. However, there are a further 30 buy-ins. Thus the total pool becomes $8000. Typically in such an event, first prize would be 50%, i.e. $4000.

The objective of the casino is to get the players back into action as soon as possible. A satellite tournament may only last a couple of hours. The blinds are usually small at first, but then they increase rapidly. Once the forced bets become a high percentage of your chips, the skill factor is substantially diminished.

Nowadays there are quite a number of players who never play money poker. They prefer tournaments for the reasons mentioned above.

Tournament Strategy

The objectives of tournament play are quite different from money poker. In the latter you can walk away from the game any time you like. If you lose your money, you can pull up some more. The object is to win as much money as you can while losing as little as possible. In a tournament you are playing for chips, not money. You want to win all the chips.

Tournaments have two contradictory objectives. First, you want to last as long as possible. After all, if there is nobody left, you have won the tournament. Second, you also need to win all the chips. Thus you must put them at risk.

Every time you go all-in in a tournament, you are risking your 'life'. In money poker you can simply beckon for more money. Thus ideally you want to set your opponents in rather than they set you in. It is better to attack a shorter stack of chips than yours. Obviously you cannot always do this. You may be dealt aces at Hold 'Em when your opponent has more chips. You cannot shirk your responsibilities in such a situation. If you get outdrawn, that's life. You will have to wait for the next tournament, play in the side action, go out to eat or just plain sulk.

While there is life there is hope. Even one chip may be enough. I played in the World Series press tournament one year. The first prize was only $1000 but it was a freebie. All life's rich tapestry passed my way. I held 6 6 against Tony Holden. The flop was K 6 4. All the chips went in and I lost to his pocket kings. Eventually I came down to just three chips. Next hand the blinds would have eaten me up. I made my stand with J♦ 3♦. The flop was three diamonds and I never looked back. In the end I was head-up against a young actor. After I had won I asked him, for the video camera, 'I've been playing poker for 45 years. How long have you been playing?' He looked at his watch and said, 'three hours'.

It is just no good playing too tight in a tournament. Some people seem simply to have the objective of lasting as long as possible. They find it thrilling to say, 'Stewart Reuben was busted out before me.' A satellite may only last a couple of hours. In that time you are not going to get many good hands. 6 6 and Q J at Hold 'Em may well go to war. The former has a tiny edge. Only one player will be left in the tournament after the river card. In this example, both players want to be the one to make the final raise. Then they can win in three ways: Everybody may pass; they may have the best hand and it stand up; or they may outdraw their opponents. This is equally true at money poker.

 TIP: Generally it is best to be the one to put in the last bet.

Position is of much less importance in tournament play than in money poker. Many hands are all-in before the conclusion of the pot. If you are first to speak, your best option is often to check, to pass a bet or to bet out.

If players are knocked out, they cannot steam. Thus one of the big attractions of money poker is removed. However, players do become rattled after losing several hands. If you can recognise them when they are in this mode, so much the better.

You will usually be busted out before you get into the money. If so, it is best to do so as early as possible. Then you can be get back into action in some other poker game. After all, time is money. Some players seem to play with the sole objective of getting their money's worth. Lasting is their aim. Naturally they can be bullied out just like any soft, tight money player.

You are likely to meet more strangers in a tournament than in your regular game. Thus you have to concentrate more on how they play. In money games I often switch off completely when I am not involved.

This is not an option in a tournament.

In tournament play it is of paramount importance to know the chip position of all your rivals. This is important in money poker only against your opponents in the hand. The financial situation of the other players is temporarily irrelevant.

For example, in a tournament two of you have $1,500 left and the third player only $300. The last thing you want to do is confront the other big chip leader. You want either yourself to pick off the little guy or for the other two to go to war. Then there are three possibilities: you become chip leader; you are slightly wounded; you win second place at no risk. You will then still have a shot at first with $1,500 against $1,800, which is not a big handicap.

You hold $1,000 when eight of the other players hold $10,000 or more. The only other player has only $400 left. The tournament pays nine places. Your first objective is to outlast that little guy. After that, you can work on building up your chip position. If he has to put in the blinds before you, just wait him out.

Many players seem to dislike playing short-handed poker. I find it difficult to understand why. If you play heads-up, then you are involved in every pot. That is a better use of your table money than sitting around watching others play. The only downside is that it is more tiring. The only way to avoid short-handed poker in tournaments is to be knocked out. You have to learn the relative value of hands when there are few players in the pot. At Hold 'Em with 10 players, A♣ 7♥ is junk. Three handed it can be solid gold.

When there are re-buys some players keep going all-in repeatedly and buying in again. Then, when they have built up a decent stake, they quieten down. It has been known for such players to have to win the tournament in order to break even. Their objective is the trophy rather than to maximise their profits. The strategy against such steamers is to wait for good hands and hope to pick them off. Be careful not to be caught in the intermediate stage where they have built up a good tank. Also don't squeal if they out-draw you. Just re-buy and grit your teeth.

Generally it is mathematically sound to re-buy. Your probability of winning is diminished because you have few chips. On the other hand, they are now worth more than at the beginning of the tournament, because there is more money to win.

At the beginning of the tournament the buy-in might be $1,000 and the betting structure $20-$40 blinds. Everybody has 25 big bets and it is possible to play proper poker. Towards the end of the tournament you may have mustered $20,000, but the blinds may now be $1,000-$2,000. Thus you have only 10 big bets. Every round it is going to cost you $3,000 if you pass every hand. If you sit and wait, you will go broke eventually. What is more, it will not be long before the blinds go up to $2,000-$4,000. Thus you must be selective, yet aggressive.

Your chances of winning the tournament improve every time somebody is knocked out. This is true even if the money goes to another player. Thus a player is all-in for small money. Now you want there to be many players in the pot in the hope that someone will knock him out.

You should never leave a short-stack with a few chips left. Always set him in, even though you think your chances are poor. Otherwise you may win but still leave him the opportunity to build up and become a threat later on.

It is very important to bluff, particularly in no limit and pot limit. Remember, your opponent wants to conserve his chips just as much as you do.

It may seem, from the tone of this chapter, that all tournaments are no limit or pot limit. This is not true in North America. Many games are played limit. Eventually the betting structure becomes very large relative to the chip position. Then the game becomes similar to the other forms. In limit being tight and aggressive is probably even more important. You must avoid frittering away part of your stack on weak hands.

Satellites present other problems. Let us assume that we start with $1000 of chips and the blinds are initially $10-20. They will go up every 15-20 minutes. Thus each pot at the start is only a tiny percentage of your stake. Half of the entrants have no chance. You should play extremely tight at first, risking nothing, and waiting until the dust has settled. Of course, if you have a good hand, you must try to pick up some ammunition.

By the time of the second increase in the blinds, you will probably be down to five players. Now you will have to play some poker. Pretty soon, if you do well, it will be down to three players and a virtual crap-shoot.

Satellites usually pay only one place for 10 players. Thus it is no use lasting and coming second. You need to win all the chips. If you have $5000 you would prefer to be up against four opponents each with $1250 than one opponent with $5000. Finishing in fifth position is no worse than finishing in second. Thus in a satellite you may go from being ultra tight to ultra loose in the space of two hours. It is not easy to make such adjustments.

Play in Hold 'Em tournaments revolves very much around how you play A K, K K or Q Q. A A is easy, you are going all-in. K K, you expect to plunge in, although it becomes a marginal hand after the second raise. The alternative is to await the flop and switch off if an ace appears. Q Q is well worth the second raise in the middle stages. If called, you are probably going to lose if an ace or a king comes. If you have A K and are facing the second raise, you are trying to outdraw your opponent, or split the pot with him.

A baby pair is very similar to a drawing hand such as 10♣ 9♣. You want to be in late position and not invest more than 5% of your stack. Sometimes you will make the second raise. This is a semi-bluff and may well secure the prize even against a medium pair.

In a poker tournament you cannot get up from the table during play. Otherwise you will lose chips in antes or blinds. If you are not present for your blinds, then they are put up for you and the chips are wasted. If you miss hands in which you do not have to post blinds, then you are losing a free roll.

Finally, there are 'comfort' stops every couple of hours. Make use of them. Wash your face. Go outside for five minutes and get some air. Relax and don't spend your time gossiping about your bad beats. Don't turn up at the beginning of the tournament half asleep, bloated from food or drunk. That is a waste of money. It would be better not to enter the tournament at all.

Where to Play

Casinos and Other Venues

When you are starting out it is ideal to play with friends who are also new to the game. The overheads are much lower playing in private games, but it may be difficult to locate a group of like-minded people. Also it is hard to keep a game going. Even so, such games can be most fun. Be careful lest you be infiltrated by strangers. Even a small game may attract undesirable elements.

In the US many forms of institutionalised gambling used to be banned outside Nevada. Thus you could only legally bet on such things as the horses and state lotteries. Nowadays several states have legalised gambling, especially on the Native American Reservations. The greatest centre remains Las Vegas. You will also find action all over Nevada, in Atlantic City, California and such casinos as Foxwoods in Connecticut.

Personally I do not like Atlantic City. It has all the sleazy aspects of Las Vegas, without the chutzpah. On the other hand, it is a magnet for a huge conurbation, providing an excellent source of new money, which is so essential in a poker game.

Many people play tiny poker in Las Vegas. $1-4 limit Seven Stud games are spread all over town. These games are populated by the elderly, out-of-towners and people who just enjoy poker. The rake is very high, possibly $10 per hour per seat. I reckon I could make $60 a day from such a game because the standard is so low, but that may be my ego talking. You must play very tightly to have a positive expectancy. Realistically, $15-30 Seven Stud is about the minimum game in which to win a useful sum. The rake is about the same and thus much smaller as a percentage.

Oddly one thing has hardly changed since I started going to Vegas in 1964. There is usually only one card room spreading big games in town. At the time of writing this is The Bellagio Resort, although that is quite likely to change. At the Bellagio games often go up to $600-$1,200 and there may be two or three $80-160 games. Seven Stud remains the most widely played form, but Hold 'Em, Omaha Eight or Better and Razz are also spread. Limit is much the most popular form, but if you turn up and are a big enough punter, the locals will oblige you with any game. Sadly I do not get this type of action. The sister resort, The Mirage, has mainly medium-sized games and also runs tournaments.

There are many rooms dedicated to poker in Los Angeles and other parts of Southern California. Casino gambling is illegal, but it is accepted that poker is a game of skill. There is also another blessing: smoking is banned.

Many casinos in Britain now have a card room. If they do not, the management may be able to tell you where the action is at. Poker is to be found in many of the Grosvenor or Ladbrokes Casinos. A detailed listing is available on www.poker-in-the-UK.com. Invariably you have to join the casino 24 hours before you are allowed in. The objective is presumably to check for undesirables. There is no charge for membership.

The two London casinos that spread poker are:

Grosvenor Victoria, Harrowby Street, London W2 from 2pm daily

Cash games varying in size from £50 Seven Stud to £1000 half Omaha, half London Lowball. Formal tournaments have now returned.

Ladbrokes Regency, Imperial Hotel, Russell Square

Cash games up to £100. Friday night is beginners' night with a £10 buy-in tournament, with a maximum of three re-buys. £3-£6 limit Hold 'Em is also spread. A number of other small buy-in tournaments are also organised during the week.

European players are referred to *Poker Europa* magazine (33 Parkhurst Road, Torquay TQ1 4EW, England) which appears six times a year and has details of activity in Europe. Their web site is www.european-poker.co.uk.

Internet Poker

This is a very recent innovation. Playing for real money only started with Planet Poker at the beginning of 1998. It is perfectly reasonable to play chess this way, but it seems to me to be the very antithesis of poker, since you cannot see how your opponents are reacting. However, many people enjoy it and there is the tremendous advantage that a game is available at any time of the night or day.

You can play mock games for play-money. For a beginner this may be very sensible, since the costs then are just connection and site charges. This is not supposed to be real poker. However, you can use it to improve your technique. This might include: betting, evaluating your hands and those of your opponents, the grammar of poker and figuring your odds rapidly. I am told that the play looks very realistic. Your first visit to a casino card-room must be intimidating. Everybody is experienced and seems to know everybody else. Low limit players often get impatient with tyros. Games are often self-dealt and this is certainly a non-trivial skill. Play-money games may help to rub off the rough edges of your play.

Playing on-line for real is fraught with danger. For example, the casino may go bankrupt, and it is therefore advisable not to leave more in your account than you can afford to lose. Also, two or more players may play in collusion and theoretically everybody in the game except you could be in the same room. Don't let me paint too gloomy a picture though. A certain amount of paranoia about cheating is always healthy at poker. Examples of sites at the time of writing include:

www.planetpoker.com

www.actionpoker.com

www.paradisepoker.com

www.24hpoker.com

www.pokerpages.com

www.highlandsclub.com

www.4knightspoker.com

Inclusion above does not in any way indicate my approval or disapproval.

www.sr.ultimatebet.com is coming online in 2001. It is headed up by some very well-known names. These include past World Series winners Russ Hamilton, Phil Hellmuth and Mansour Matloubi. They intend to run a very tight ship. Pot limit and no limit will be introduced to the web for the first time. Players will be able take part in really tiny stakes tournaments, perhaps as low as 25-50 cent. The level will also go much higher than is currently offered elsewhere. They then intend to extend their operation to other games, always with an emphasis on betting.

Strategy

Your opponents will not be paying the charges to pass. Avoid making their mistakes, do not get sucked in on junk. Bluffing is not an option. Just bet and raise and keep on at it when you have a good hand. Deception will not be noticed. Change your handle (the name by which you are known) from time to time.

Good luck. These five lines should be enough for a winning strategy.

Poker Education and Entertainment

The cost of books or software is negligible in the scheme of things. Just one idea in a poker book may compensate you for the cover price of the work. The main investment is in time. Can you afford the several hours required to read and digest a book? It may be that you have read material in this book with which you disagree. That can only be good. It means that you are thinking critically for yourself.

Some players are totally contemptuous of reading material, saying 'I've nothing to learn from theory. Poker is a purely practical game.' Well, I've learnt from writing this book and I hope that I will always have something to learn from somebody else's opinions. Otherwise I will be dead – at least from the neck up.

Why should a practical poker player offer sound advice? That is easy to answer for a work like this. We need to see fresh blood in the game. Explaining the basics helps popularise the game. As mentioned earlier in this book, an income stream in addition to playing poker is essential. I like writing and have tried to arrange my life so that everything I do is enjoyable.

Books for Study

Pot Limit & No Limit Poker by Bob Ciaffone and Stewart Reuben

Well, I would recommend that, wouldn't I?

Omaha Hold 'Em Poker by Bob Ciaffone

This seminal work has been tremendously influential. It continues to popularise this complex form of poker.

Improve Your Poker by Bob Ciaffone

This is mainly a collection of essays on limit poker.

The Science of Poker by Dr Mahmood N Mahmood

A highly mathematical treatment of Hold 'Em and Omaha High, bursting with common sense.

Poker for Dummies by Richard Harroch and Lou Krieger

Like most of the 'for Dummies' series, this is no such thing. It is for bright people who know little about the subject.

Poker, A Guaranteed Income for Life by Frank Wallace

This is full of sound advice. Its prime value is the insight it gives into how a manipulative, conniving schemer thinks about the game.

All material by Dave Sklansky is well worthwhile.

The series by Two by Two Publishing, which includes works by such writers as Mason Malmuth and Ray Zee, is extremely worthwhile. These are mainly technical works.

Championship No-Limit & Pot-Limit Hold 'Em and *Championship Omaha* both by T.J. Cloutier and Tom McEvoy

These are highly readable anecdotal accounts of how to play these games, mainly in tournaments. T.J. and Tom, Bob and I all decided independently and simultaneously, that books on no limit and pot limit would serve poker well.

Super System – A Course in Power Play by Doyle Brunson, together with Bobby Baldwin, Mike Caro, Joey Hawthorne, Chip Reese and Dave Sklansky

This massive tome contains a wealth of useful advice. Its prime message is – be aggressive.

Books for Fun

These are all a wonderful read and will also make excellent presents for non-players.

Big Deal by Anthony Holden

An account of Tony's one year as a professional player.

The Biggest Game in Town by Al Alvarez

The definitive account of the World Series of Poker.

Total Poker by David Spanier

David was a life-long friend. This is his personal view of our great game.

The Little Book of Poker by David Spanier

A collection of David's articles from his weekly column in *The Independent*, a national British newspaper.

The Hand I Played by David Spanier

A memoir of David's love affair with poker, published posthumously.

At one time or another Tony, Al and David all played in the 'Tuesday Night Game' to which I was somehow never invited.

The Education of a Poker Player by Herbert O Yardley

This classic, first published in 1957, is still essential reading. It contains a little theory mixed in with immensely enjoyable anecdotes.

The Cincinnati Kid by Walter Tevis

There has been surprisingly little fiction written on poker. This is the best known and deals well with some of the psychology, particularly that of a loser.

Shut up and Deal by Jessie May

I am not enamoured with this portrayal of the poker scene. Jessie assures me that the work is fiction.

Magazines

Card Player Magazine (3140 South Polaris Avenue 8, Las Vegas, Nevada 89102, USA)

This appears monthly and carries a great deal of information on public card rooms. Their web site is www.cardplayer.com.

Poker Digest Magazine (1455 E Tropicana Avenue, £300, Las Vegas, Nevada 89119, USA)

This appears every two weeks. Their website is www.pokerdigest.com.

Films

The Cincinnati Kid starring Steve McQueen and Edward G. Robinson

Quite fun, but I wish my opponents would play poker like this. Did its influence cause me to set myself up as 'the man' to beat?

Maverick the TV series and film

The heroes from James Garner to Mel Gibson are always professional poker players. They gladden my heart because they are usually fairly upright, but tricky citizens.

The Odd Couple by Neil Simon starring Jack Lemmon, Walter Matthau

This very funny play and film is set around a private poker game.

The Sting starring Paul Newman and Robert Redford

Poker is only an aside, but the movie is wonderfully evocative of old con games.

California Split starring Elliott Gould and George Segal

This is about gambling, especially on horses. The poker scenes are particularly authentic.

Rounders starring Matt Damon

This is all about the compulsive and sometimes destructive nature of poker. No real human being is simultaneously as good and bad at the game as the hero. In fact, there is a technical error. The young hero doubles up and doubles up in a heads-up game. He ends up with more than four times his start money. I wonder if anybody else noticed?

The Hustler starring Paul Newman

This film about playing pool remains the best film ever made about poker. This is despite the fact that it has nothing whatsoever to do with the actual game. It is all about winning and losing.

The theory that compulsive gamblers want to hurt themselves is often offered. In my experience it is very rare. I only remember one player who could visually be seen to get sexual gratification from losing.

Late Night Poker Channel 4 Series on British Terrestrial TV.

I always knew a poker series would make compulsive television viewing. However, I was never able to persuade a TV executive of this. The format is that all the players buy in for £1500 (just over $2000). They then play tournaments in groups. The winner of each group goes through to the final. It is thus a standard Hold 'Em tournament, except that there is a climax at the end of each episode. Hold 'Em is much the best game to show. It is easy to follow what each player holds. Some time after filming, it occupies a slot once a week for several weeks.

The game is played on a very large table which is transparent from below. Cameras below the table are able to show the viewers what each player holds. The programmes were only started in 1999 and it is thus hardly surprising that techniques are still being developed. I believe that too little attention is paid to the chip position of each player. Odds are seldom quoted. But the main defect is that there is too little interaction with the players. Viewers want to hear a player explode with outrage when he has just been outdrawn. The banter in a poker game is always fun. Why not interview the players at the end of each episode? Jessie May and Nic Szeremeta are the presenters and we hear too much of them. Understandably the producer fears that viewers will not understand what is going on.

I am delighted to report that the series so far broadcast have been extremely successful. They have attracted high viewing figures despite the late hour. My criticisms are meant to be constructive comments on a series that is still being developed.

Dave (Devilfish) Ulliott has become something of a celebrity since winning the first series. The future of poker in Britain has never looked rosier.

Theatre

Dealer's Choice by Patrick Marber

This is very much about an English private game. It is no coincidence some of the players seem like people I know. The author studied the Grosvenor Victoria regulars.

Music

The Gambler sung by Kenny Rogers

'You've got to know when to hold'em, you've got to know when to fold'em.' Rogers even made a TV series around such a gambling man. One episode featured the same set piece hand as *The Cincinnati Kid*. At least this time it makes sense. Also Kenny wants to pass, but is nagged into calling by his backer.

Deuces Wild an album by Frankie Laine

All 12 numbers relate to gambling, some to poker

Software

Nothing dates a book so much as recommending the white heat of new technology. I am sure that the software available will help improve your poker and provide some fun. You do not need to be a techno-whizz. Otherwise I would have been left helpless at the starting gate. You should have at least Windows 95 on your computer, although DOS or earlier versions of Windows may possibly do.

Wilson Software (PO Box 4087, Pinetop, Arizona 85935) have produced user-friendly software on Hold 'Em, Omaha High, Omaha High-Low Split and Seven Stud.

Naturally, after a time, play against a computer palls. It is difficult to create programs which will react flexibly to the human user. You will learn how to outplay the machines. If you don't, perhaps you are not ready to spend your money in live action in casinos. I am not going to tell you how to beat them. It should be fun and instructive finding out.

In the early 1980s I prepared material for humans to play computers at poker for Radio-Shack (Tandy). I doubt that the software can still be obtained, but it was a great deal of fun. My associate David Levy played his first hand of Hold 'Em against the program. The flop was A♦ K♦ J♦. He held Q♦ 10♦. 'What should I do?', he asked after the computer checked. 'Check', I recommended. The turn they again both checked. On the river David perforce had finally to bet. The computer passed. Now, that is what I call a bad beat story. To hit the 650,000/1 best hand and then win nothing at all.

The game 'World Series of Poker' enables you to play as if in the $10,000 buy-in World Championship at Binion's Horseshoe. It is fun to play against. It took me several hours, spread over several days, to win the series.

The Wilson software can also be used to do computer simulations. These can certainly help to determine precise odds of an all-in coup. Simply deal out 50,000 hands in a couple of minutes and look at the results. In Omaha or Seven Stud, it is difficult to make precise calculations with several cards to come, and it is virtually impossible to visualise all the possibilities. For example, in real life I once had (A♣ 4♣) 2♣ at Seven Stud. My final hand was A A A A 2 2 4, and I managed to get paid.

You can use different styles to see how they fare. Is it true that soft, loose is a sure loser? Of course such a simulation is not the real thing. However, it may help to clarify your thinking.

Video Poker

Let us be clear on something. *This is not poker at all.* It is a slots game where you aim to make poker hands instead of perhaps three cherries in a row. Interestingly enough though, it is one casino game where you may be able to win. Deuces wild used to pay out 100.25% against perfect strategy. Have the casino managers gone mad? No, they figure that most players will have heard that the machine can be beaten, but will not play optimally.

A dollar progressive is even more interesting. Every time a player puts in a dollar, the jackpot goes up by one cent. If the jackpot has not come up for a long time, then the machine will have a positive expectancy. You must always play the maximum number of coins, as this essential in order to be paid the jackpot. I have met professional slots players who are always on the look-out for such machines.

These machines do not exist in Britain.

Caribbean Stud Poker

This is a casino game which again simply uses the values of poker hands. The house takes a massive 5%. Do *not* play this game. It will seriously damage your pocket.

Enough about these gambling games. They annoy me, taking the name of poker in vain.

Chapter Twelve

Glossary

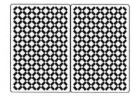

A schoolboy asked me to include a list of poker expressions, as he felt lost hearing all sorts of terms which were unfamiliar to him. It started as a glossary, and has turned into a mini-dictionary, but however extensive it is, it can never be complete. In compiling it, I have accessed other lists, such as sr.ultimatebet.com. No doubt other authors will use this one. Fair enough, I only hope that they acknowledge the source. The etymology of specifically American slang words has not been indicated.

According to Hoyle The correct rules. (Hoyle wrote a book explaining card games, possibly before poker was ever played.)

Action The activity that takes place in a pot.

Action Hand One likely to cause a great deal of activity.

Advertise To spend money on bluffing in the hope of getting later strong bets called.

Aggro (British, Contraction of aggravation). To annoy your opponents deliberately.

Ainsworth 6 2.

Ajax A J.

Alabama Knight Riders K K K.

Alexander K♣.

All-in To bet all the chips or money you have left on the table.

All o' dem Your opponent declares jacks at the end of the pot. 'How many?' 'All o' dem.'

American Airlines A A.

Ammunition Chips.

Angle Tricky, unethical play.

Ante A compulsory stake from all the players before the deal.

Apple Biggest game in a club.

Argine Q♣.

Arkansas Flush Four flush.

Baby A low card such as a five, four, three or two. Particularly used in games with a low.

Backdoor To make a hand in Hold 'Em or Omaha using the last two board cards.

Back into See backdoor.

Back-raise. To re-raise, usually after first checking.

Back to Back In Stud a pair with one card in the hole and the other showing. For example, Five Card Stud (A♦) A♣ or Seven Stud (9♥ 3♦) 9♠.

Bad Beat To lose a pot very much against the odds. There must be more bad beats than good beats, because nobody ever tells me about the latter.

Bad Beat Jackpot A sum of money awarded for the biggest bad beat. When rolled-over, it can become anti-poker. The jackpot may exceed the pot.

Badge (British) See buck.

Bad Shape To have little chance of winning the pot.

Bankroll The money you have available with which to play poker. Bankroll + nut must never exceed your worldly wealth.

Barbara Hutton 10 5. (She owned Woolworth.)

Baskin-Robbins 3 A. (They have 31 flavours.)

Beat the Board Having a hand that can only beat any hand that is in sight in Stud.

Beer Hand 7 2.

Belly Buster An inside straight, for example 9 8 7 5 and hit a 6.

Betting Interval The stage during a hand where each active player is entitled to check, bet, raise or pass, depending on the situation. It ends when the last action has been called by all the players still left in the hand.

Betting on the Come Betting in the expectation of making a hand with cards to come.

Bicycle 5 4 3 2 A.

Big Bet Poker Pot limit or no limit.

Big Blind The largest bet made by a player before the cards are dealt. This is often compulsory at Hold 'Em for the player two to the dealer's left.

Big Slick A K.

Bitch Q.

Black Maria Q♠.

Blank A card in a flop game which comes on the turn or river and helps nobody.

Blind (1) The first bet made by a player before the cards are dealt. This is often compulsory at Hold 'Em for the first player to the dealer's left.

Blind (2) To check or bet without first looking at the cards you have or before you receive a new card.

Blivit A worthless hand.

Blockers Cards which make it less likely that your opponents hold a straight. For example, you have A 9 9 4 in Omaha. The flop is J 10 8. A straight is unlikely.

Blocky 6 3.

Blow Back To lose back the profits.

Blue Chip The largest denomination chip used to be blue in colour. This is the origin of the expression 'blue chip stock'. Nowadays it is more usually black.

Bluff To bet or raise with a hand you believe to be losing.

Board The cards showing.

Boat A full house.

Bobtail Straight An open-ended straight draw such as 9 8 7 6.

Bombe Atomique (European) A tremendous hand. For example, holding A♠ A♥ Q♣ 10♥ with a flop of A♣ K♥ J♥.

Bottle (1) (British) 2. (Rhyming slang; bottle of glue = two.)

Bottle (2) (British) To be courageous.

Bounty Cash prize offered in tournaments for knocking out a certain player.

Boxed Card A card which is accidentally face up in the deck.

Boy J.

Brassic (British) To be broke.

Bring it in To make the first bet.

Broadway A K Q J 10.

Broderick Crawford 10 4. (What he said into his radio on *Highway Patrol*.)

Broomcorn To lose all the money in antes. Named for the eponymous Mr Broomcorn.

Brush Man The person in charge of the seating.

Brutal Outdraw.

Buck The moving button, used when there is just one dealer, to indicate which player receives cards and acts last.

Bug A limited wild card. At Draw High it can be used only as an ace or in straights or flushes.

Bullet A.

Bully Johnson 5 3.

Bump To raise.

Bundle A large sum of money.

Buried Having lost all your money.

Buried Hadens Aces in the hole at Seven Stud. For example, (A A) 9. David is one of the best limit Seven Stud players.

Buried Pair A concealed pair in Stud.

Burn To take off the top card face down before dealing. The purpose is to help prevent cheating.

Business To save money when all the betting is done, but there are still cards to come. This is frowned on in Europe, but popular in the US. It slows down the game.

Busted Broke.

Busted Flush (or **Straight**) Four to a flush which failed to catch the fifth of the suit.

Button See buck.

Buy-in The minimum amount required to play in a particular game.

Buy the pot To bet a large sum in order to win the pot.

Caesar K♦.

Cage The casino area where you exchange money for chips or vice-versa.

Calamity Jane Q♠.

Call To match the previous bet.

Calling Station A player who always calls, never passing or raising.

Call or Pass One player in a pot limit or no limit game may be allowed to play this way. It means he is prepared to cover whatever anybody else has on the table.

Call the Police (British) 9 9 9.

Call the Police (US) 9 A A. In both cases the number one dials for emergencies.

Cap To make the last permissible raise at limit when there are more than two players in the pot. Usually only three or four raises are allowed.

Card Rack Somebody thought to hold unusually good cards.

Caribbeanist (not used in America) Somebody who plays ultra-tight.

Carpet (British) 3.

Case Card The last available card of either a denomination or a suit.

Case Money The last money you have available. Never find yourself in this situation.

Cash In or **Out** To leave a game and exchange your chips for the folding stuff.

Catch To hit the card or hand you needed.

Changing Gear Going from playing tight to loose or vice versa.

Charles K♥. (King Charles VII of France.)

Chase To call a hand in the hope of improving, usually against the odds.

Check To take no action in the pot at this stage, reserving the right to pass, call or raise if other players bet.

Check Blind To check without looking at your hand.

Check Dark As check blind.

Check-raise First to check and then to raise when bet at.

Checks (US) Chips.

Chemmy Shuffle To spread the cards face down on the table, then to shuffle them there. (Derivation from Chemin de Fer, a card game similar to Punto Banco.)

Chinese Poker This is not poker at all.

Ching (British) 5.

Chip The counters representing money of various denominations.

Chip and a Chair Having few chips, but still being in the tournament.

Chip-declare A High-Low game. After the betting, each player indicates whether he is going high, low or both, with chips in his hand.

Chip Race Small chips eventually become unnecessary in a tournament. They are then changed up and the odd ones left over drawn for.

Chip Runner Staff member who obtains chips for you in exchange for your cash or cheque.

Chop it up To divide up or split the pot.

Cinch A hand that cannot be beaten.

Clock the Action To determine what is going on in a hand.

Coconuts See nuts.

Coffee-housing An attempt, by words or actions, to confuse the other players in the pot.

Cold A bad run of cards over a period.

Cold Call To call a raise and re-raise, having taken no action in the pot previously.

Cold Deck A deck of cards brought in by a cheat and not shuffled.

Collars up (British) To be very short of cash.

Columbia River K 7.

Come To call or bet in the hope of improving later.

Community Cards The cards in Hold 'Em or Omaha which can be used by any player.

Comp Short for complimentary. Where casinos offer players incentives, such as free meals.

Computer Hand Q 7.

Connectors Consecutive cards such as Q J or 9 8 7.

Cop and Hop To leave immediately after scoring a win.

Count-down Determining what a player has bet when he has gone all-in.

Counter-bluff Raising with a poor hand when you think your opponent may be bluffing.

Counterfeited Where a board card matches one of your cards, thus rendering it useless. For example, you hold A Q J 2 at High-Low Omaha. The board is K 7 3. Now a deuce comes on the turn. You have been counterfeited and hold no low.

Coup The total action of a whole hand.

Cover the Table To have more money on the table than anyone else.

Cow To pay half a buy-in and then receive half the return.

Cowboy K.

Crabs 3 3.

Crack To beat a powerful hand.

Cripple To hold the cards others require.

Crying Call To call, because of pot odds, not expecting to win.

Curse of Mexico 2♠.

Curse of Scotland (British) 9♦.

Cut (1) After shuffling, to divide the deck into two sections and then put the previous bottom half on the top.

Cut (2) To decide the seating arrangements in a game.

Cut (3) The money the house takes from the pot.

Dame Q.

Dangler Card in Omaha unrelated to the other cards. For example, K♣ Q♦ J♦ 4♥. The 4♥ is a dangler.

Darth Vader 4♠ 4♣. (Dark fours.)

David K♠. (King David.)

Dead Card A card which is no longer in play.

Dead Cards A Stud hand with few chances of improving because of the cards passed.

Dead Hand A hand which is no longer in play, possibly due to an irregularity.

Dead Man's Hand The hand Wild Bill Hickock is supposed to have been holding when he was shot in the back. It is A♠ A♣ 8♠ 8♣. The fifth card is unknown.

Deal (1) The act of giving each player his cards.

Deal (2) Reaching an agreement on splitting the pot or the money in a tournament.

Dealer's Choice A form of poker in which each player, in turn on his deal, chooses a game of his own preference.

Deal it out Twice A way of reducing the fortuitous element of cards to come when all-in.

Deep The money is deep when players in the pot have bundles on the table.

Deuces Twos.

Devil's Bedposts 4♣.

Dime $1,000. That's inflation for you.

Discard Pile The cards that have been thrown away.

Dog To be odds against in a pot.

Dog Balls 8 8.

Dollar $100.

Dolly Parton 9 5. (As in the film *Nine to Five*.)

Door-card The first up-card in a Stud game.

Double Belly Buster A hand where it is possible to make two inside straights. For example, Seven Stud (9 8) 7 J 5. Both a 10 and a 6 make a straight.

Down Card Cards received at the end of the pot face down, particularly in Stud.

Doyle Brunson 10 2. (The hand with which he won both the 1975 and 1976 World Series.)

Do your Pieces (British) Lose all your available money.

Drawing Dead Drawing to a hand which cannot win.

Drawing Out To make a hand by drawing card(s), particularly when holding a mediocre hand.

Drawing Thin Playing with few cards to improve to win.

Driving Seat Said of a player in a Stud game whose face cards seem to give him the best of it.

Drop To fold.

Ducks Twos.

Dunce Connection 5 3 2 off-suit in Stud.

Duplicated See counterfeited.

Dust Action by a dealer when leaving a game to show that he has no concealed chips.

Dwell To think a long time before taking action.

Early Position One of the first three players in a flop game.

Elk River Trip 10s.

Equity The amount of money you can win in the pot.

Eubie 8 6. (As in, if you play these you be broke.)

Eyes A A.

Face Cards Up-cards in Stud.

Fade To survive bad luck.

Family Pot One in which most of the players compete.

Farm To bet all your chips.

Favourite The hand which is most likely to win.

Feeler Bet A small bet to determine where the land lies.

Fever 5 or bet of five.

Fifth Street The fifth card in Seven Stud or sometimes the last card of a flop.

Fill Up To make a full house.

Filth (British) An utterly mediocre hand.

Finky 8 5.

Fire To bet a large amount.

Fish A weak player.

Fish-hooks J J.

Flat Call To just call a bet.

Flimp the Pot (British) To put too little money in the pot.

Flint to Saginaw Trip 10s. (Apparently it is 30 miles between these two towns.)

Floorman The card room employee in charge of the game.

Flop The first three communal cards in Hold 'Em or Omaha.

Flopping a Set To make trips on the flop using two cards from your own hand.

Flush Five cards of the same suit.

Fold To throw away one's hand.

Four Flush Four cards of the same suit.

Four Flusher A cheat as in, 'you dirty rotten four flusher'.

Four of a Kind Four cards of the same denomination.

Fourth Street The fourth card in Stud or sometimes the fourth card of a flop.

Free Card To receive a card without there having been a bet.

Free Roll The situation where you are splitting the pot. However, cards to come may give you and only you the winning hand.

Freeze Out A game which must continue until only one player has all the chips.

Friendly Game There is no such thing as a friendly game of poker.

Full House A hand containing trips and also a pair.

Funnies Complex games with wild cards.

Gamble Usually means to wager. It is often used pejoratively, but not in poker.

Garden (British) 8. (Rhyming slang; garden gate = eight.)

Gay Waiter Q 3. (Queen trey.)

GHM (British) Going Home Money. A small sum of money given by the house to a player who has gone broke.

Gilroy Trip 10s. (San Jose to Gilroy is 30 miles.)

Girl Q.

Going South Removing money from the table and putting it in one's pocket even though not in a pot. This is illegal especially in pot limit or no limit. It is even worse during a hand.

Going to the Table Putting all your money into the pot.

Good Shape To have a good hand.

Good Shot Often said through gritted teeth when you have just been outdrawn badly.

Gooley (British) £1,000.

Goolsby Q 10.

Gorillas K K. (King Kong.)

Grand Jury Trip 4s. (There are 12 on a jury.)

Graveyard The shift in a casino from midnight to 8am.

Gravy Unexpected profit.

Gut-shot A middle-pin straight.

Half Pot Limit Poker where you can bet only half the pot.

Hand (1) The cards you hold as a player.

Hand (2) The whole action in the pot from deal to showdown.

Hart, Schaeffer and Marx Trip jacks.

Heads-up A game involving solely two players.

Hector J ♦.

High-Low A form of poker where the best high and best low hands split the pot.

High Roller One who gambles, usually casino games, for large sums.

Hit To make a winning hand.

Hit-and-run Merchant Somebody who leaves immediately after winning a pot.

Hockey Sticks 7 7.

Hold-out To retain concealed cards with a view to using them later. This is utter cheating of course.

Hole Cards Concealed cards in stud.

Holy City The nuts.

Horse To play five forms of poker: Hold 'Em, Omaha Eight or Better, Razz, Seven Stud, Seven Stud Eight or Better.

House (1) A full house.

House (2) The organisation running the game for a table charge.

House Player One who plays for the organisation.

Hughey, Dewey and Louie Trip deuces.

Ignorant End (mainly Omaha) The low end of four to an up and down straight. Thus a flop of 9 8 2. You hold K Q 7 6. The five is the ignorant end, as a ten does not give you the nuts.

Implied Odds The odds you expect to get in a pot caused by other players calling or, of making your hand and being called.

In the Dark To check or bet blind, either without looking at the cards or before fresh ones are dealt.

In the Middle To be between a bettor and a potential raiser.

Inside Straight Four cards such as 9 8 6 5.

Insurance A side bet to ensure that you do not lose all your money. Illegal in Britain.

Isolate To drive all but one opponent out of the pot.

Jack Benny 3 9. (This was the age the comedian always claimed to be.)

Jackpot A sum of money provided for the best hand of the evening.

Jam To raise and re-raise.

Joe Bernstein 9 3.

Joker A wild card that can be used to represent anything.

Judge Benn Trip 10 s.

Juice The percentage taken by a bookmaker or when offering insurance.

Katie K 10.

Kibitzer A spectator, often one who comments on the play.

Kicker The side card(s) to the hand. For example, Seven Stud (K 7) 7 then the king is a kicker.

Kick it Up To increase the size of the game.

Kill As played in limit High-Low split. The blinds are $75-150. A player scoops the whole pot. Then the next hand he must go $150 blind in addition to the two forced blinds. The hand then becomes $150-300.

Killer Cards Those which reduce your opponent to perhaps one out. For example, in Omaha you hold A♥ A♣ Q♥ 4♦. Flop K♥ 7♥ 2♠. A♠, A♦ are killers on the turn.

King Crab K 3.

Knave J.

Kokomo K 8.

Lady Q.

Lancelot J♣.

Late Position Hand seven or later at Hold 'Em.

Lay Down To throw away one's hand.

Leaners See connectors.

Lenny 3 5 off-suit.

Light To owe money in the pot. Sometimes done deliberately as a form of cheating.

Limit Poker when played with bets fixed in size.

Limp In To call cheaply late in hand.

Line-up The players in a game.

Live Cards Where your improving cards in Stud have not been seen.

Live One A weak player.

Lock A hand that cannot lose.

Loose Play possibly in defiance of the odds.

Lowball Poker where the lowest hand wins.

Lumberman's Hand 2 4. (A two by four plank.)

Make a Ricket (British) To make a mistake such as betting out of turn.

Make the Deck To shuffle and prepare the deck ready for dealing.

Man with the Axe K♦.

Mark Somebody who is going to be cheated.

Marked Cards Where cards are marked to indicate what they are. This is the best-known form of cheating, but it is not so easy to do.

Marker An IOU.

Marriage K Q suited. (From Pinochle.)

Maverick Q J.

Mechanic A cheat who arranges the cards in the deck.

Middle Pin A card such as 8 in the sequence 9 7 6 5.

Middle Position Hands four to six in Hold 'Em.

Mighty Wurlitzer 8 8.

Milk To bet small in order to encourage a call from a hand with no chance.

Misdeal Where a hand is dealt incorrectly and has to be dealt again.

Miss the Flop Where your cards have no relationship to the flop.

Molly Hogan Q♠.

Mongrel K 9. (Canine.)

Monkey £500.

Montana Banana 9 2.

Moody To misrepresent your hand by play-acting.

Motown J 5.

Move in To bet or raise your opponent all-in.

Moves (British) To make a complex play in an attempt to win a pot.

Muck (1) See discard pile.

Muck (2) To throw away your hand.

Mystery A new card that helps your hand but looks useless.

Nail To win big against your opponent.

Neves (British) 7.

Nickel $5.

No Limit Where the player is allowed to bet or raise any amount he has in front of him. This is irrespective of the size of the pot.

Nut The money needed to pay one's overheads, For example, mortgage, food, clothing.

Nut Flush The best possible flush.

Nuts The currently best hand.

Octopus Ten to call. (Tentacle.)

Office Hours 9-5 straight.

Officially Steaming Supposedly to be playing with the intention of steaming.

Off-suit Cards of different suits.

Ogier J♠.

Oldsmobile 9 8.

One-eyed Jacks The two jacks shown in profile.

O'Neil Bet The blinds are $50 $50. In pot limit the first bet is in the range $50-200. $150 is an O'Neil bet. (Named after O'Neil Longson.)

On the Come Where betting in the hope of improving.

On their Backs To show the hole cards when all-in.

On Tilt To play badly after losing badly.

Open (1) To initiate the action with a bet.

Open (2) Loose and usually aggressive.

Open-ended Straight See bobtail.

Openers In Draw poker the cards you use to open, e.g. J J.

Option The right of the blind to raise.

Outdraw To receive a card making your hand better than your opponent's.

Outs The cards which may turn your hand into a winner.

Over Bet To bet much more than the pot in no limit.

Over-cards Cards higher than the flop cards which, if they come, pair you up.

Overlay Up-cards, such that, with the best possible hole cards, the hand would be winning. (? ?) 9♠ 4♥ 3♦ 4♣ overlays (? ?) 9♣ A♣ 7♣ Q♣ because it may be a full house.

Over the top To raise a player's bet.

Paint Any picture card.

Pair Two cards of the same denomination.

Pallas Q♠.

Pass (1) To fold.

Pass (2) (in the US) To check. Be careful, such ambiguity can lead to trouble.

Pat Hand A hand at draw where no cards are bought.

Phase The level of action in a game. Phase 4 is lift-off. Players are willing to pour their money in with scant regard to poker values.

Phil's Hand 9♠ 9♣. (Phil Hellmuth won the World Series with this hand.)

Pickle Man 5 7. (Heinz.)

Picture Card K, Q or J.

Piece of Cheese A very weak hand.

Pinochle Q♠ J♦.

Pips The symbols on non-court cards.

Play Back at To re-raise.

Playing Over To take the place of a player temporarily absent from a cash game.

Play the Board In Hold 'Em to use only the board cards at the end of the pot.

Playing the Pot Out To be prepared to call, bet or raise all bets at limit poker.

Play Over Box. A transparent box covering the chips of a player being played over.

Pocket A pair in the hole. For example, Seven Stud (9 9) 7.

Point A.

Poker (Irish) Quads.

Poker Face Giving nothing away from the expression on your face.

Pony £25.

Pop Group J J 5 5. (As in Jackson Five.)

Position Your seat at the table relative to the bettor.

Post If absent from the table, you may be required to make up the blinds missed.

Pot The money or chips at stake in the hand.

Pot Limit A form of poker where the maximum raise is the size of the pot *after* calling.

Pot Odds (Size of the pot)/(Size of bet to call).

Presto 5 5.

Previous As in previous convictions. To have done something before that suggests you will do it again.

Price The odds you are receiving to call a bet.

Prile Trips.

Proposition Player One paid by the house to make up games but who plays his own money.

Punter (British) A gambler.

Puppy Feet Clubs.

Push To split a pot.

Put down To fold.

Put You On To believe you hold a particular hand.

Quads Four cards of the same denomination.

Qualifier Where in High-Low there is an upper limit set on the low. For example, eight in Omaha Eight or Better.

Quartered-off Where you receive 25% of the pot in High-Low.

Quinine Q 9.

Rabbit Hunting Looking at the cards to come after the pot has been passed out. What a waste of time! Sometimes disgracefully done before the conclusion of the pot.

Race See chip race.

Rachel Q♦.

Rack A small tray in which chips are held.

Rags (Stud) Low cards not connected to the hand.

Railbird A spectator, often one who cannot afford to play.

Railroad Hand J 6.

Rainbow Three or four suits so that a flush is impossible.

Raining Discreet comment to draw the presence of an obtrusive kibitzer to the attention of the dealer.

Raise To put in more money than the previous player.

Rake A percentage of the pot taken by the house.

Rap To knock the table, indicating taking no action.

Raquel Welch 3 8. (Possibly her measurements.)

Rat-hole See going south.

Read To try to figure out what cards your opponent(s) hold.

Readies (British) Available cash.

Re-buy (tournaments) To buy new chips.

Re-draw Your opponent receives a card which outdraws your previous hand. Now you receive a card which beats his hand.

Release To throw away your hand.

Represent To check, bet or raise in order to give the impression of a hand of different strength from that actually held.

Re-route To change direction with your hand. Holding Q♦ 9♦. Flop 10♠ 8♦ 4♣. Turn 3♦. You are now trying to make a flush as well as a straight.

Reverse Dangler For example, K 9 8 7. The king is a reverse dangler.

Ring Game A table where there is no empty seat.

River The last card to be dealt in a hand.

Road Game The most reliable form of poker for you to win at.

Rockets A A.

Rock An extremely conservative, usually also strong, player.

Roll To have a good run of cards.

Rolled up In Seven Stud to have trips in the first three cards.

Roll me Over Instruction to the house when offered a seat. This indicates that the next person on the list should take the seat. However, one wants to stay on the list.

Rouf (British) Four. (Reverse the first and last letters.)

Rough A low hand where the secondary cards are high. For example, 8 7 6 4 2.

Rounder A strong professional player.

Royal Flush A K Q J 10 all of the same suit.

Royal Low The best low. 7 5 4 3 2 or 6 4 3 2 A or 5 4 3 2 A depending on the game.

Ruck (British) To have a row.

Run (1) A straight.

Run (2) A series of either good or bad hands.

Rush A run of good hands.

Salvatore Bluff Betting with a very strong drawing hand. For example, holding at Seven Stud (A♥ Q♥) K♥ J♥ against (? ?) 9♣ 2♠. Jim Salvatore used indeed to be a very tight player.

Sandbag To check with the intention of raising if somebody else bets.

Santa Barbara A K.

Satellite A tournament, with perhaps eight players, where you can win the buy-in to a bigger tournament.

Save In a two-handed pot, to come to an arrangement to save perhaps the last bet.

Scare Cards Cards which come later in the hand which are worrying.

School The players in a regular poker game.

Scoop To win all of a High-Low hand.

Scourge of Scotland 9♦.

Scramble the Deck See chemmy shuffle.

Scratch (British) To have only a small amount of money.

Second Nuts The second best hand.

Seconds The second card from the top of the deck that is dealt by a mechanic as if the first card.

See To call.

Semi-bluff To bet a hand which may or may not be winning or which may improve later.

Set Trips.

Set you in To bet all your opponent's remaining chips.

Shill A house player staked by them to make up the game. He receives a small wage.

Shoot it up To raise.

Shop To reveal the strength of your hand by your betting.

Short-handed Game One with few players.

Short Stack A pile of chips, belonging to a player, of relatively little value.

Showdown To display your cards at the end of the hand.

Showing out To cheat by indicating your hole cards to a partner.

Show one - show all If you reveal your cards to one player after a pot, you must show them to the whole table.

Shuffle To mix the cards preparatory to dealing.

Shy To owe money to the pot.

Side Action Money games that take place in the same period as tournaments.

Side Pot When one player is all-in, betting may continue. The money he cannot win is the side pot.

Siegfried and Roy Q Q.

Simultaneous Declaration See chip declare.

Sixth Street The sixth card dealt in Seven Card Stud.

Skin To win all of a player's money.

Slippery Anne Q♠.

Slow-play To check or bet small, without intending to raise, to represent weakness.

Slow-roll To display your hand slowly, particularly first showing one weaker than that of your opponent. Naturally this is appalling manners.

Small Blind The first compulsory blind after the dealer.

Smooth The opposite of rough.

Smooth Call To call a bet in multi-way action.

Snatch Game (US) One where the rake is excessive.

Snowman 8.

Splash Around To bet frequently.

Splashing the Pot To fire chips into the pot, possibly less than announced.

Split Where the money in a pot is split between two or more players.

Split Openers A player opens at Jackpot Draw with K♥ Q♥ Q♦ J♥ 10♥. He discards the Q♦ and draws to the straight flush.

Split Pot One where two or more players share the pot.

Spread To provide a particular version of poker.

Spread Limit Betting where the limit is with a range, for example

$1-$5.

Squeeze (1) To look at the extremities of your hole cards. This may be done to prevent others peeking, or to maintain the tension.

Squeeze (2) To bet so that it is difficult for the next player to call, because of what later players might do.

Stand Pat To decline to take cards at draw.

Stay To remain in a pot by calling.

Steal Position Late position where it is reasonable to bet with a weak hand to steal the pot.

Steam To play over-aggressively often after losing a big pot.

Steel Wheel 5 4 3 2 A suited; a five high straight flush.

Stopping Bet A small bet made to discourage a big bet when you don't know where you stand.

Straddle The last blind before the deal.

Straight Five consecutive cards, not of the same suit.

Straight Flush Five consecutive cards of the same suit.

Strangulation Coup A hand where one player has the absolute nuts.

Streak A run of either good or bad hands.

String Bet Where a player puts chips in the pot and then reaches back for more in order to bet or raise more. This is illegal.

Strip Poker Where the players play for items of clothing rather than money.

Stripped Deck A form of poker where the cards two through six are removed from the deck.

Stuck Losing.

Stud Each player receives separately cards face down and, in addition, cards face up.

Suicide King K♥.

Suited Connectors Connected cards of the same suit, for example, 8♣ 7♣.

Sweat Where a railbird is rooting for a player to win.

Sweeten To raise the pot, often by a small amount.

Table (1) The piece of furniture on which poker is played.

Table (2) The players in the game.

Table Charge The amount charged per hour.

Table Stakes Where a player cannot put more money in the pot than he has on the table. Pot limit and no limit are always played this way. See call or pass.

Table Talks (1) High-Low where, after betting, the players show their hands and the best high and low split the pot.

Table Talks (2) Where a player shows his hand, but under-declares it, the true value of the hand stands, if noticed.

Tank Your money on the table.

Tapis (French) To go all-in.

Tapped To go broke or all-in.

Tell A mannerism which indicates the strength of a player's hand.

Terrible Shape To have very few chances of winning the pot.

Through Ticket A hand which ensures that you will play through to the end. For example, trips in limit Seven Stud.

Tight A player who only plays strong hands.

Tilt See steam.

Time (1) The amount of table charge collected at specific times.

Time (2) Sometimes spoken by a player who wants to think about calling *or* raising and does not want to confuse his opponents.

Tip your Hand To reveal the quality of your hand.

To do your Pieces To lose all your money.

Toke A tip to the dealer. (Sadly, illegal in Britain.)

Trap As in, for example, trap seven, meaning seat seven.

Trap-check To check with the intent of causing an opponent to bet, thus allowing you to raise.

Trap Hand One which, by its nature, causes you to lose money.

Trey 3.

Trips Three of a kind of the same denomination.

Turn The fourth communal card at Hold 'Em or Omaha, sometimes also card four at Stud.

Twiggy 2 9. (Her measurements.)

Two Pair (1) Such as 9 9 4 4 Q.

Two Pair (2) Players sometimes call quads this way. Unethical if the hand isn't shown immediately.

Underdog A hand, with cards to come, that is not likely to win.

Under-raise To raise less than the previous bet. In the US this is only allowed when going all-in. In Britain it is only permitted when going all-in or in a two-handed pot.

Under the Gun The first person to bet in a flop or draw game.

Union Oil 7 6.

Up Card At Stud, a card in a player's hand which is open.

Utility Bet One which may serve several functions, for example driving players out, determining the strength of the opposition.

Value The amount of money that can be won, relative to the amount to call.

Verbal To mislead by talking.

Vigorish The percentage taken by a bookmaker. See rake.

Waiting in the Weeds To be lurking with the intention of raising.

Wash To have broken even, or an even money situation.

Weed (British) See going south.

Weinberg 10 3.

Wheel See bicycle.

Wicky-wacky-woo 2 4 6 8 10 (From the Benny Hill Show.)

Wild Card See joker.

Wired Three of a kind in three cards in Seven Stud.

Wooden Hand One with no win.

Woolworth's A form of poker where all the five and tens are wild. (The 5 and 10 cent store - see Betty Hutton.)

Wrap or **Wrap-around** A hand in Omaha where it is possible to make many straights. Consider a flop of 7 6 2. 9 8 5 4 is a complete wrap with 20 outs.

Yeast Raise.

Yiddisha Forest Three 3s.

Zone The area in your mind of understanding what is going on.

Chapter Thirteen

Solutions to Exercises

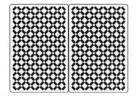 

Chapter One: Solutions

1. A flush.

2. One in two hands.

3. The pot is $30 before he acts. He calls $10 and thus can raise $40.

4. 52.

5. The amount of money with which you commenced the hand.

Chapter Two: Solutions

Points are allocated for each answer.

	limit		pot limit		limit			pot limit		
	C	B	C	B	P	C	R	P	C	R
1.	10	5	10	2						
2.					0	6	10	2	8	10
3.					4	10	0	10	3	0
4.	10	2	10	1						
5.					10	6	0	10	2	0

Note: C, B represents Check, Bet; P, C, R represents Pass, Call, Raise

Comments

1. Basically it is too likely there is someone out there with a better hand.

2. A pair of aces is not that great, but it figures to be winning, except against a really tight opponent.

3. In limit you probably have your odds to draw to a four flush. You are clutching at straws if you call at pot limit.

4. Normally you should check when facing a caller who drew one card. If he has two pair, he should bet. If he is on a draw, what is the point in betting?

5. Things have gone terribly wrong. You called to make a hand and now all hell has broken loose. If you call, there would probably be yet another raise. You would probably continue to call just in case all your opponents should be locked up. Throw away your hand. If it would have won, just smile gently.

Score

100   Well done.

80-99   Your game just needs a little fine-tuning.

60-79   Your are not yet ready to play in a big poker game.

40-59   It would be best to reread the chapter before moving on.

0-40   Would you like to play some poker?

Chapter Three: Solutions

	limit		pot limit		no limit		limit			pot limit			no limit		
	C	**B**	**C**	**B**	**C**	**B**	**P**	**C**	**R**	**P**	**C**	**R**	**P**	**C**	**R**
1							0	5	10	10	6	1	10	4	1
2a							10	4	0	10	1	0	10	0	0
2b							5	10	0	10	10	0	8	10	2
3	9	10	10	2	10	5									
4							0	3	10	0	8	10	0	6	10
5							0	3	10	0	7	10	0	10	8

Note: C, B represents Check, Bet; P, C, R represents Pass, Call, Raise

Comments

1. In limit there is no reason to think you are losing. It is better to raise than call. Otherwise players with weak hands are more likely to limp in. You are only 9/2 against making trip kings if somebody does have aces. In pot limit or no limit it is time to bow out gracefully.

2. 9S 8C is a moderate drawing hand. It should be passed in early position. In late position you might even fancy a raise as a bluff, provided the money is very deep. There is little point to this at limit.

3. You are probably beaten. At limit it is better to bet than check and call. If you intended the latter, slap yourself on the wrist. Soft play is seldom to be recommended. It is not that terrible a play at the big bet games to semi-bluff.

4. You have a magnificent drawing hand. It may be even better two-handed. Go for it!

5. You made a pretty atrocious call on the flop, even at limit. Fortune has smiled on you. It is desirable to raise now to clear away the dead-wood. If you come up against K Q, it is your fault for calling on the flop.

Score

180	Are you quite sure that you did not peek at the answers?
140-179	Excellent.
100-139	Okay, but remember that every mistake costs money.
60-99	You need to reread this chapter carefully.
0- 60	Your parents warned you not to do your homework and watch TV at the same time!

Chapter Four: Solutions

	limit		pot limit		limit			pot limit		
	C	B	C	B	P	C	R	P	C	R
1a					2	10	0	10	10	0
1b					10	10	0	10	2	0
2a	3	10	3	10						
2b					3	10	0	8	10	0
3					0	10	1	10	2	0
4					0	4	10	0	7	10
5					0	10	1	10	2	0

Note: C, B represents Check, Bet; P, C, R represents Pass, Call, Raise

Comments

1. I am not going to try to persuade you to pass three to a straight flush. The hand is too seductive at limit. It is much too expensive even at limit after so much action in the second case.

2a. Whenever you take the initiative, there is a chance that everybody may pass. Or you may hit an open pair next card and frighten everybody out. Also that straight is a pretty good shot.

2b. You are looking down the barrel of a gun. A raise is quite likely and the pot may cost you dear. Yes, this can also be true of limit poker.

3. In limit you have a good chance of outdrawing two pair. In pot limit you are petrified that he has mystery trips. If he is bluffing, he is a very advanced player.

4. Most likely you have trapped him. The worst case scenario is a straight. You have many ways to beat that. Two pair is another possibility. If your opponent was chancing his arm with a pair of jacks, then you will probably push him out. That's a pity, since he has only two winning cards *and* you have many ways to improve.

The problem arises at pot limit if he now re-raises. The pot will then be huge and you have 12 outs from 42 cards. Odds of 5/2. You do not want to stir up action, if you are afraid of a raise and have a big draw. Oddly enough, it would have been a better raise without the four flush. Then, if he re-raises, you can pass without a care in the world. You have only four outs.

5. This is a crying call at limit. The odds are too good to pass up. He may have misread the situation and have only two pair.

Unless he is a weak player, he has you beat at pot limit. Surely he is not getting busy with a flush. After all, you have raised an open pair. Occasionally, you will be wrong to pass.

TIP: Only weak players are never bluffed out.

Score

140	Well done.
120-139	Excellent.
80-119	There is no room for complacency.
50-79	Please play against me.
0-50	Your understanding of the game needs more work.

Chapter Five: Solutions

	limit		pot limit		limit			pot limit		
	C	B	C	B	P	C	R	P	C	R
1a					0	10	8	0	10	5
1b					0	7	10	0	8	10
2a					0	10	0	10	3	0
2b					0	10	0	10	5	0
3ai	10	0	8	10						
3aii					10	5	0	10	0	0
3bi	10	8	10	1						
3bii					10	4	0	10	0	0
4a	10	8	10	4						
4b	0	10	9	10						
4c	5	10	4	10						
5					0	10	8	2	10	0

Note: C, B represents Check, Bet; P, C, R represents Pass, Call, Raise

Comments

1. For both hands you should either call or raise. Both are much too good to pass and should sometimes be raised. You do not have to fall in love with aces single suited.

2. Pass both hands in pot limit. You are probably up against aces and, in the first example your hand is severely limited, while in the second you would have preferred Q J 9 8. In limit you must play.

3. Hand ai) is worth a bet in pot limit. You have the blockers that make it difficult for anyone else to have a straight. Also you have four nut outs with a ten. It is better to check in limit. You cannot expect to win every hand.

aii) A bet is a bluff, just hoping that nobody has anything. If raised you must pass and lose your chance at quad eights.

b) Your hand is pretty hopeless in both cases against a bet.

4a) Either bet or check. You are desperate for action, but it is unlikely that anybody will lead out without the straight. Checking will only secure you a small pot. You could win a great deal with a bet – but it is unlikely.

4b) You are unlikely to be called by a poor hand. Yours is easily outdrawn and you may only be sharing the pot at the moment. There is much to be said for checking the flop.

4c) You have a splendid drawing hand and betting will give the impression that you have the straight on the flop. You are favourite against anybody who has just K 10.

5. Although your flush is small, you well be winning. He may not even have noticed that there is a backdoor flush, which has happened to me. Then they turned up with the better flush, to their own amazement, blast it! If you do raise at limit, he may re-raise. Then you must make a crying call. At pot limit you can only afford to pass against the 'Rock of Gibraltar'.

Score

230-240	Congratulations. You have graduated.
200-229	A very good result.
160-199	Satisfactory.
120-159	Resist playing for high stakes.
80-119	You have not grasped the principals of Omaha.
0-80	Well, Omaha is a difficult game.

Chapter Six: Solutions

		Razz	London Lowball	2-7	A-5+Joker
1.	pass	10	10		
	call	4	1		
	raise	0	0		
2.	check	10	10		
	bet	3	2		
3.	pass			10	10
	call			1	0
	raise			0	0
4.	pass			0	0
	call			10	5
	raise			10	10
5.	check			10	10
	bet			5	2

Comments:

1. Pass in both cases. The eight may get you into trouble.

2. Check in both cases. You are an 11/10 underdog with two cards to come. On sixth street, if your opponent does not improve, you would like to go all-in.

3. Pass in both cases. You have inadequate odds to improve. Remember that your opponent(s) may also improve.

4a. You are sufficiently strong to consider slow-playing your hand and just calling.

4b. You need to re-raise. This hand is too easy to outdraw. If you are run over by a better hand, then you are going to have to go to the cage.

5. Check in both cases. You must give your opponent room to bluff. In no limit you might consider a small bet. You are representing a stopping bet, as if you are afraid of a big over-bet. Trying to behave like a quivering jelly does not come easily to a good player. This is one case where you may succeed. If he passes, the illusion will be complete.

Score

100	I am getting jealous.
80-99	Excellent.
60-79	You need to do more work.
40-59	Could do better.
under 40	Unlucky?

Chapter Seven: Solutions

	check		bet		pass		call		raise	
	limit	pot	limit	pot	limit	pot	limit	pot	limit	pot
1a					10	10	0	0	0	0
1b					0	0	10	8	8	10
1c					0	0	4	4	10	10
1d					10	10	1	0	0	0
1e					10	10	1	0	0	0
2.					0	0	0	2	10	10
3a					0	0	10	8	8	10
3b					2	10	10	5	0	0
3c					2	5	10	10	0	0
3d					10	10	5	10	0	0
3e					0	0	10	10	2	0
4a	10	10	10	10						
4b	2	2	10	10						
4c	10	10	7	4						
4d	10	10	8	6						
4e	6	8	10	10						
5a					0	10	10	4	0	0
5b					0	0	0	5	10	10

Comments

1. In a), d) and e) your hands are all mediocre. Throw them away.

In b) and c) you have premium hands. If your opponents want to go all-in, by all means join in the dance.

2. Your hand is vastly better than trip kings. You have two cards to make a straight flush, seven more to make a flush (three of which give you a lock for low), six more to make a straight (three of which also give you a lock for low) and nine more to give you a lock for low. A call is slow-playing your hand.

3a) You hold the ultimate hand. There is little point in telling your opponents this in limit. No opponent is going to pass because of the extra raise. Pot limit you may be able to move players out.

3b) This is okay at limit, but it is more discrete to pass at pot limit.

3c) This is a premium hand and should be played. It is true that you will often lose. However, you will also be a frequent winner.

 TIP: There is no shame in passing.

3d). This is a dreadful hand. Both aces may be out. Pass, even though you know you are not losing at this stage.

3e) This hand is much too good to consider passing. However, it is no longer exciting.

4a) This hand is so good you can certainly trap check.

4b) This hand is not strong enough to slow-play. It is very strong. However, you do not want to share the low, unless you win all the high.

4c) This is an unusual hand, designed mostly for limping in at limit. However, a bet would be misleading at limit.

4d) You have nothing for high. A bet constitutes a bluff. There is nothing wrong with that occasionally, even at limit.

4e) This is very strong for high and not too bad for low. You do not want to see a low card on the turn.

5a) It will be a miracle if you receive more than a quarter of this. That is okay for a call at limit. You should have passed earlier at pot limit.

5b) This is strong. It would be timid just to call even at pot limit.

Score

360	Wow!
310–359	Extremely good.
260–309	You should be good enough to win.
200–259	There is still a great deal of work to be done.
140–199	High-Low really is very complicated.
80–139	You are not good enough to consider playing for money – except against me!
0–80	How did you do in the other sections?

Chapter Eight: Solutions

1. a) 0; b) 5; c) 10.

2. a) 0; b) 10; c) 5.

3. a) bac 10; b) bca 5; c) abc 5; d) acb 2; e) starting with c 0.

4. a) 10; b) 2; c) 0.

5. c) 10; d) 8; b) 4; a) 2.

Score

50	You are on the same wavelength as me.
40-49	Excellent.
30-39	Satisfactory; poker is not a science.
10-29	You lack understanding in certain principles of poker.
0-10	Oh, dear!

Chapter Ten: Solutions

Figures have been approximated to make them easier to remember. Score 10/10 if you approximate to the figure shown. If you are far out, score 0.

1. a) 19/20; b) 6/5; c) 11/4

di) pass 5; call 2; raise all-in 10

dii) pass 10; call 2; raise all-in 7

2. a) 3/2; b) 4/1

ci) pass 0; call 10; raise 9

cii) pass 0; call 10; raise 2

3. a) evens; b) 19/10

ci) pass 0; call 4; raise 10

cii) pass 0; call 7; raise 10

ciii) pass 0; call 6; raise 10

civ) pass 0; call 9; raise 10

4. ai) 3/1; aii) 5/1; aiii) 11/1

bi) pass 3; call 10; raise 2

bii) pass 6; call 10; raise 0

5. a) 7/4; b) 5/2; c) 4/1

di) pass 10; call 6; raise 2

dii) pass 10; call 2; raise 0

diii) pass 10; call 2; raise 0

div) pass 10; call 0; raise 0

Comments

1. There is little point to calling. You may fail to get on if you make your flush. If you raise, in money poker you may be winning, you may bluff him out or outdraw him. If you lose, you can pick yourself up, dust yourself off and start all over again. In a tournament why risk your life on a tenuous situation?

2. Note, hand b) is more dangerous to you than trips. It blocks five of your outs. You want to encourage callers with your hand. The only hand you really want to pass is J 10. Thus why raise and drive away the pigeons? However, a raise constitutes a semi-bluff and you may well win the pot. At money poker you can stand a re-raise.

3. You have a premium hand. What is more it looks like a flush draw. If you raise and hit a diamond, he will probably pass. If you make your straight, he may well call. The only reason for cooling down in a pot limit tournament is that you may go broke on the hand.

4. Do not get over-excited by what is, after all, just a drawing hand. You do not even have your true odds before the flop. You are, perfectly reasonably, relying on implied odds.

5. You have a terrible hand. First you will have to make your flush. Then you will have to hope that the board does not pair. Then you will have to hope that no third low card falls. The proper place for this hand is the muck.

Score

270	Really? Please don't play in my games.
230-269	Terrific.
190-229	Very good.
150-189	Perhaps your arithmetic let you down.
100-149	There must be one game you do not understand.
0-100	I am surprised that you read through this chapter. It was not really essential.